THE
TUGMAN'S
PASSAGE

THE TUGMAN'S PASSAGE

EDWARD HOAGLAND

RANDOM HOUSE · NEW YORK

Copyright © 1976, 1977, 1978, 1979, 1980, 1982 by Edward Hoagland
Map Copyright © 1982 by Anita Karl

All rights reserved under International and Pan-American Copyright conventions. Published in the United States by Random House, Inc., New York, and simultaneously in Canada by Random House of Canada Limited, Toronto.

The essays in this work, some in different form, first appeared in the following publications: *American Heritage, Harper's, The Nation, The New York Times Book Review,* and the *Sierra Club's 1981 Wilderness Calendar.*

Grateful acknowledgment is made to the following for permission to reprint previously published material:
Brandt & Brandt Literary Agents: "Johnny Appleseed" from *A Book of Americans* by Rosemary and Stephen Vincent Benet (Holt, Rinehart & Winston, Inc.). Copyright 1933 by Rosemary and Stephen Vincent Benet. Copyright renewed © 1961 by Rosemary Carr Benet. Reprinted by permission of Brandt & Brandt Literary Agents, Inc.
The New York Times: Previously published editorials by Edward Hoagland from *The New York Times* editorial page. Copyright © 1979, 1980, 1981 by The New York Times Company. Reprinted by permission.

Library of Congress Cataloging in Publication Data

Hoagland, Edward.
The tugman's passage.
I. Title.
PS3558.0334T8   814'.54   81–15803
ISBN 0–394–52268–0   AACR2

Manufactured in the United States of America
24689753
FIRST EDITION

FOR MY MOTHER AND FATHER,
AND FOR MY GRANDMOTHER MORLEY
AND GRANDFATHER HOAGLAND

CONTENTS

Walking the Dog / Stuttering Time / The Cost of Fur / In the Spring / Chiaroscuro / Love Story / There Go the Clowns / Mountain House / Swamp Ensemble / The Bittern Boometh / Songs and Snakeskins / Complex Justice / Tug of Sweet Trout / The Prime of Life / In the Woods / North Country Diary / Stars to Eat / Summer Pond / The Roar of the Moon / In the Paws of the Surf / Fire Worshiper / Deadly Colors / Labels versus Life / Barking Geese and Butternuts / City Pebbles / Heel and Toe / Rattlesnake Stakes / Cold Males, Neo-females / Banking for Winter / December Song

.

THE
TUGMAN'S
PASSAGE

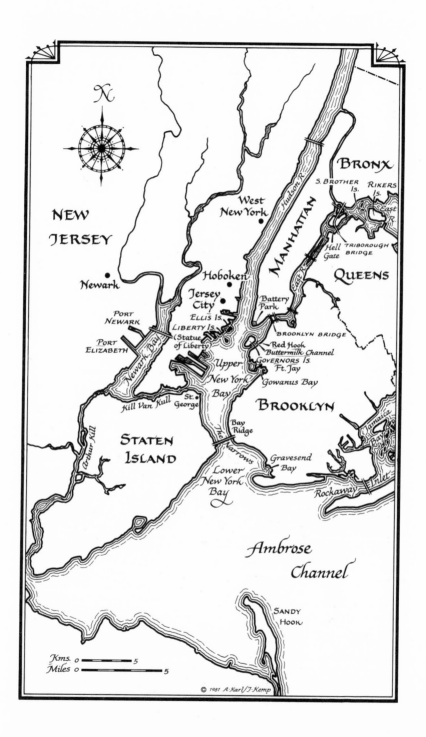

N

NEW
JERSEY

West
New York

Newark

BRONX

S. BROTHER
IS.

RIKERS
IS.

East
R.

Hell
Gate

TRIBOROUGH
BRIDGE

Hoboken

QUEENS

MANHATTAN

Hudson R.

Jersey
City

PORT
NEWARK

Ellis Is.

LIBERTY IS.
(Statue
of Liberty)

Battery
Park

PORT
ELIZABETH

Newark Bay

BROOKLYN BRIDGE

Red Hook
Buttermilk Channel
GOVERNORS IS.
Ft. Jay

Upper
New York
Bay

Gowanus Bay

Kill Van Kull

St.
George

BROOKLYN

STATEN
ISLAND

Bay
Ridge

The Narrows

Jamaica
Bay

Arthur Kill

Lower
New York
Bay

Gravesend
Bay

Rockaway
Inlet

Ambrose

Channel

SANDY
HOOK

Kms. 0 ———— 5
Miles 0 ———— 5

© 1981 A. Karl/J. Kemp

THE
TUGMAN'S
PASSAGE

Captain Artie Biagi, of the
Moran Towing Company, broke into this organization of
mainly Irish tugboatmen in New York harbor more than
thirty years ago, when he was a young man job-hunting
with a hangover. By a fluke, he fell into conversation with
an individual in the adjoining booth of the men's room at
Maritime Association headquarters near the Battery. He
couldn't see the fellow, but—in that day more innocent
than our own—after they had chatted awhile about his getting drunk the night before at the Red Men Lodge in West
New York, New Jersey, and about his previous jobs in a
tar yard and driving a laundry truck and as a deckhand on
an army tug that had gone clear to Baffin Island, in Canada,
he learned that his companion was a magnate of the shipping industry. Another tug captain of Italian ancestry—at
that time a runaway from an orphanage, hanging about the
docks on the Lower East Side—landed his first job when a

paternal Irishman took pity on him and let him "ham" on his boat, working at first for just his meals.

Biagi's mother was German, and his father's mother was Scotch, so it's an accident of American sociology, he says, that he is called "Italian." Round-faced, soft-chinned, he is laconic on the bridge of a ship when giving directions for its docking, but then talkative when he gets back to the wheelhouse of his tug. Ten years ago, when I first went out on the water with him, he was servicing the S.S. *United States*, the English *Queens*, and the *Raffaello*, as well as the usual miscellany of tramp freighters and harbor barges, from a big 4,300-horsepower tug called the *Teresa*. Now, close to retirement, he has the 1,200-horsepower *Christine*, and a lighter schedule of two days on and two days off, and a crew—mate, engineer, cook, and deckhand—each man of which is full of memories. Bobby Perlitz, the deckhand, is so gimpy after forty years of working on the waterfront that, to oblige him, Biagi uses a flimsy ladder Bobby can still manage to lift for the risky business of climbing from the *Christine* to the decks of the ships Biagi docks.

New York's port, when strike-free, is the busiest in the country, with more than seventy-five hundred arrivals in the course of a year. Opposite Sandy Hook, which curves into the sea from New Jersey to form the sheltering lip of the outer harbor, every ship picks up a pilot, who guides it up the channel, past Gravesend Bay, through the Narrows between Staten Island and Brooklyn, under the Verrazano Bridge, nearly seventeen miles altogether, to the Battery in Lower Manhattan—though most ships now will turn aside a little before that. They may tie up in the bleaker reaches of Brooklyn, or else head on around Staten Island, past Robbins Reef, Constable Hook, Sailors Snug Harbor, and Shooters Island in Kill Van Kull, up Newark Bay to the extensive new facilities for containerships in New Jersey, much more accessible to interstate truck traffic than the congested old streets of Manhattan's waterfront.

A tug or two will assist at tight passages and in the actual docking, before which Biagi or another tugboat captain will have boarded the vessel and assumed the responsibilities of the Sandy Hook pilot. The tugboat deckhands have heaved up their lines to the ship's seamen in the meantime. These seamen are a worldly, various assortment of Japanese, Indonesians, Germans, Slavs, and Danes, and peer silently over the railing as the "monkey's fist"—the weight at the end of the rope—flies up to them. Fresh off the ocean, they look windblown, wet, and foreign, and they are tongue-tied with the tugmen, as the tugmen are with them, but as high as they are, they have a vigorous air, a forecastle fellowship with one another, yet also a sightseer's eagerness in new territory.

Biagi, spruce on the bridge, where there are always intimations of the nineteenth-century social order, radios instructions to Red Nordberg, his mate, in the *Christine*'s wheelhouse—"Come ahead slow," "Come ahead full," "Easy back"—which Nordberg, who is often out of sight of the ship's bridge under the flare of her bow, confirms by tooting on the tug's whistle. Before the era of walkie-talkies, this sort of communication was done from the bridge of the ship with a police whistle, and if there was a second tug, working at the stern, also the ship's whistle. Before radios were used in the harbor at all, a tug had to take a run past the company's office at the Battery after completing a job, and the dispatcher shouted the next assignment through the window with a megaphone. If the message was more complicated he waved a towel, and the tug captain tied up and went to a pay phone. Still further back, before there were such luxuries as offices and telephones, rival tugboats simply sailed out to Gravesend Bay at dawn and bargained against each other from ship to ship.

Both Biagi and Nordberg, whose brush-shaped red moustache swallows most of his smiles but who, even so, looks boyish, have won citations for bravery displayed in water emergencies. Over the years, they—like Richard Decker, the shy, fastidious engineer, who comes from a long line of Staten Island oystermen—have rescued people scalded in boiler explosions and sailors swimming between patches of blazing oil. They have seen people drown after being accidentally jostled off the Staten Island ferry, and many grayish, eel-gnawed bodies of suicides and murder victims. Once Biagi was bent over the bitt on a barge moored under the Brooklyn Bridge when there was a tremendous splash right next to the bow. He whipped around and noticed a white object rising underwater. It looked like some kind of ball, but he realized it was a bald head, instead. Mournfully the man's face bobbed out of the water. He was alive, still conscious. Their eyes met. "I want to die," he said, very calmly, because Biagi had started to kick off his workboots. Then the current caught him, in the sudden way it has in the East River—six knots strong—and gave him his wish.

Like most tugboatmen, all the *Christine*'s crew are family men, their children now grown up; that was why they never went to sea. Only the cook, Leo, has been divorced. Leo Catarina, born in the Philippines, is agile and thin, with a crouching posture that he has probably developed from stooping in so many galley hatches to peer out at the water and up the sides of big ships. He fills in as an extra deckhand occasionally, and though he wears a dashing, drooping moustache that makes him look younger than the others, and though he recently married a young Italian girl in Brooklyn who has given him a new baby who is the light of his life, outdoors he appears frail. His favorite stint, he says, was a period of years he spent cooking on a little tug on Lake Champlain, taking his son along sometimes for the trolling they did from the fantail as the boat pushed a barge. In the spring they might have a frost, and the tug would crunch through, breaking virgin ice—ice so clear and new it shattered like crystal a hundred yards ahead of them.

At lunch, Leo, serving chicken, liked to ask me, "Do you want white meat, dark meat, or Filipino meat?"—which I took to be the forestalling device of a man used to explaining his skin color.

Leo, and Bobby, from Rockaway, and Decker, too, calculated their exacta and box bets on the horses as they ate, the galley a clutter of *Doc's Daily Racing Selections*, *American Turf*, and *Racing Star*. Decker, who got his start on the water in 1933 as a messboy on a buoy tender, has impaired hearing—"boilermaker's ears"—from tending so many roaring diesels since then (tug engines being adaptations of railroad diesels originally, he said). Like other engineers I had encountered, he seemed slightly skittish, as if the deafening solitude of the engine room might accentuate the quirks and wariness that any person began with. Yet, hearing of his four children and seven grandchildren, whom he flies to visit on vacations, I realized that tugmen lead double lives. Most of them insist upon the point, and regale each other with tales of their soft berths at home.

Seamen, too, lead lives that are far-flung, sharply divided. But many tugboatmen go back and forth twice a week from the desolate, salt-stained piers of Red Hook to mow the lawn in some eminently domestic suburb of the city.

7

Some keep a second, hideaway household in one of the five boroughs as well. Pulling hawsers half the night, backs aching—till they do it in their dreams for hours afterwards—and sleeping in the roar of the engine, in a dingy cabin, with a diesel galley stove, a firehose curled around the toilet in the john, they try to figure how to spend the extraordinary money some of them earn.

Biagi has seen to it that his son has also become a docking pilot (against the opposition of a few senior harbor Irishmen), and this has worked out well. Artie, Jr., in contrast to his father, is as edgy as a bullfighter. Tall, dark, gruff, and Latin, gravel-voiced, obsessed with his job, and pugnacious about it, he is a rising star in the rather nervous hierarchy of docking pilots, and Biagi, Sr., both enjoys his prominence and worries about his fits of perfectionist pique. It's not only a question of how the bosses respond to a temper tantrum, but the deckhands' reaction. Tug captains who fall off the ladder between ship and tug can be crushed or saved, according to whether the deckhand who was holding the ladder tries, in the split seconds available, to snatch the captain free of the churning water.

Artie, Jr., in a jump suit, with comb in hand, appears to be continually on show, at least to an audience of one, but he is not without humor. Dressed fussily in suede, he will stride onto an 800-foot tanker and tell the guard and the third mate, as he climbs the long staircase, that no, he's not the pilot; he is an investor who has just bought the ship and wants to inspect the bridge. In fact, it's traditional that top tugboat pilots dress spiffily—they wore dark suits, derby hats, and chesterfield coats in the old days, as Biagi, Sr., much impressed then, remembers—and that they also be contentious and jittery.

Each Biagi earned around $70,000 in 1978. After the purchase of a home in the exurbs and a fine car or two, what does one invest in? Other tugmen have sunk their funds into land development, a restaurant, stocks and bonds, a racehorse. The Sandy Hook pilots, who enjoy a similar monopoly in practicing their trade, make slightly less—a senator's salary. They may live all over, in Maine or Florida or the Carolinas, flying in and out of New York at biweekly intervals. In Artie Sr.'s case, he bought a 27-acre trailer park in the Poconos, expecting that his daughter and her husband would run it, but instead they got divorced. With the sort of energy he devoted to learning harbor charts many years ago, he has been taking flying lessons, there in Pennsylvania, living in a big empty house and studying the interesting points of instrument landing—wondering whether he might not have had a better time from the beginning if he had aimed to be an airline pilot.

Biagi has heart trouble, Nordberg is recuperating from an abdominal operation, Decker is sixty-three and fragile-looking. And so they all are full of life-and-death stories. Biagi remembers the smell of the nursing home where his poor mother, with sheepskin padding on her hips and elbows to prevent bedsores, finally died. On his index finger he bears a scar from when his daughter, as a baby, fell into convulsions and he stuck his finger in her mouth to try to clear her breathing. The doctor whose house they blundered into injected her, by mistake, with an adult's dosage of morphine; and yet she lived; she is in Texas now.

Being watermen, they have a special knowledge of tragedy and peril. The city's bodies end up bobbing in the tide, after having been mauled by the Hudson's ice all winter. And on the boats, although a hawser rarely actually snaps, if one only "jumps" off the bitt it can kill a deckhand. Or a bitt can break off, propelled like shrapnel. Not only the captain, climbing to a ship, can tumble into the rushing water between tug and ship. So can a deckhand, balanced on the rail or standing on a fender, as the tide throws ship and tug together with a hard bump. Or, if a tugboatman turns alcoholic, an oddly public drama may result. He sits on the pier under the giant Colgate clock in Jersey City, where the chandler's truck delivers grub to Moran's tugs and his old comrades are going to see him. When they swing ashore, they shake hands, give him sandwiches, maybe a coat. But he sells the coat. He's coughing. They stop again, talk to him, leave a sweater, pass a plate of food to him. Sitting once again on the frigid bulkhead next December—a figure who in better days had shared a thousand suppers in the galley—he catches the captain's eye. He is slumped over. The captain touches him. He is dead.

More ships called at New York ten or twenty years ago, but they were freighters—what are now called "break-bulk ships"—with a forest of stubby cranes to reach into the several fore- and after-holds, and they were smaller. Small shipping operators and the nautical lines of the so-called developing countries still employ these, but huge specialty ships, such as the twelve-deck car-carriers that shuttle to America loaded with Toyotas, have become the muscle of maritime commerce. There are vessels hollowed out to carry nothing but grain or scrap metal, and innumerable containerships that carry not loose cargo loaded by means of slings and pallets into holds but two or three thousand aluminum boxes that, set onto flatbed tractor-trailers, shoot off unopened to almost as many destinations. With ships built for drive-on, drive-off convenience, a minimal crew can clear the harbor efficiently in a single day if their arrival alongside the dock is timed to coincide with the longshoremen's morning shape-up.

Containerships have a simplified profile, all of the housing being at the stern; and on the Jersey piers, jumbo black cranes like dinosaurs lean over them to hasten the work. An American variation is the LASH (Lighter Alongside Ship), which transports perhaps ninety barges, instead of tractor-trailer bodies, and a 500-ton sliding derrick that rolls back and forth in order to hoist them. Again, it isn't nearly as pretty a craft as an old-fashioned freighter, but the harbor —a place of "grease," payoffs, pilferage, "piecing" somebody off, where a man that you used to notice walking along in a lumberjack shirt ("Mr. Pier Eight") might have had $20,000 in his pocket—is getting so automated that soon only white-collar crime will be left.

In Buttermilk Channel, between Brooklyn and Governor's Island, we intercepted a cargo ship, the *African Mercury*, which was painted black, red, and white, with two sea horses on the bow. The *Diana Moran* was also there, to help Biagi dock it. Because in the current the ship would have turned like a weathervane if left to its own devices, until finally the bow pointed into the "wind," or current, Biagi positioned the *Christine* and *Diana* at bow and stern to counter this eventuality and keep it broadside as it entered the slip at Brooklyn's Pier 11. A ship when broadside to the hop of the tide is like a seesaw, with its fulcrum in the middle. But as the bow slides inside the slip, escaping the current, the fulcrum naturally shifts aft. As the *African Mercury*'s bow got "lighter" and the stern "heavier," Biagi adjusted the placement and thrust of his tugs accordingly. The whole process took three-quarters of an hour, until the ship's lines to the dock were fast.

11

We then sailed the *Hellenic Splendor* from Fifty-seventh Street, Brooklyn—a much quicker operation, the ship's own propeller backing her out. The *Christine* simply fastened to her bow and acted as the rudder. Next, we sailed a Japanese boat, *Blue Nagoya*, from Pier 36, north of the Manhattan Bridge on the East River; and then the LASH *Stonewall Jackson* from Brooklyn. After lunch we rendezvoused off Robbins Reef with a neat, white-and-green, Russian-built, Kuwaiti-owned vessel, *Al Mansouriah*, managed from Liverpool and headed for Port Newark. The captain, as Biagi mentioned afterward, was an Englishman born in Argentina named J. P. Kosidowski. Because of the jumble of origins and destinations, I thought of Józef Korzeniowski—Joseph Conrad.

We were so busy because three other Moran tugs were out of commission. The *Cynthia* had hit a ship with her wheelhouse in an awkward maneuver. "She tried to push the ship with her front window," as Biagi put it. The *Margot Moran*, towing a barge, had blundered into a piling, which did no damage in itself but stopped the *Margot* dead, so that the barge she was towing rode up over her stern and hit her capstan and rear housing. And the *Elizabeth* had thrown a bolt on her reduction gear.

Late this October afternoon, as we docked the ship *Mormacaltair* in Gowanus Canal, the seamen and two longshoremen who were hauling on a stern line got careless before the ship had come to a dead halt, and the rope tangled in the ship's screw. For half an hour they diddled with it while the ship's captain, by gently reversing engines, shook the rope, and the mate and pier boss radioed back and forth as to whether a diver ought to be called. The accident would turn serious if the propeller was torn askew. In New

York the standard fee for cutting a line loose from a propeller is $300, an honorarium that many times has been collected by a tugboatman swimming underwater with no gear but the cook's meat saw and a bandanna tied across his nose.

"Isn't that the way?" I said. "One man earns three hundred dollars for risking his life, and another just the same money for picking up the phone."

"It's come in handy, though," Biagi said.

In the evening at slack tide we helped a captain named Hugo van Slegtenhorst, from Hoagland, Holland, to steer his Shell Oil Co. tanker from a tank farm opposite Riker's Island in the Bronx to Ross Terminal in Kill Van Kull. She measured seven hundred forty-eight feet long, one hundred three feet wide, and, lightened as she was, drew twenty-six feet of water. The controlling depth in the East River is only thirty-four feet, at Poor House Flats, opposite Twentieth Street in Manhattan, and so about a quarter of her load had had to be tapped off to barges before she had gone up the East River to the Bronx in the first place. On the other hand, if a ship's mast rides more than a hundred twenty-six feet high it will hit the Brooklyn Bridge (as happened recently with a tanker one of Biagi's friends was piloting), so not too much oil can be off-loaded before a trip in either direction.

Gliding south, we gazed at the storybook luxury of the Upper East Side of Manhattan almost as if we owned it. With the three-quarter moon, the cake-on-cliff buildings, beige and creamy, many lighted, some shadowy, were surpassingly beautiful. Houselights in Manhattan in their millions look glowingly yellow when seen from the river; skyscraper offices have white-lit windows; and the bridge lights are blue. The tanker, under its own steam and Biagi's guidance and with marvelous aplomb, slid the seven miles from Hell Gate to Lower Manhattan, whose intricacy of windows is even more crowded and jewellike and radiant —stunning when lit up because it is such a statement of power.

"*Wall Street*," we explained to a Dutchman who was new to New York, though by day the dense clutter of buildings does not loom as large. Jammed, hypertense, they do not really go together. Each was originally some architect's or tycoon's obsession—like a single impassioned shout— so that, looked at together, they add up to a cacophony. From a distance, however, out past the Statue of Liberty, they seem to sail on the water, narrow as a frigate.

Captain van Slegtenhorst had a crackerjack complement of officers and men on the bridge, and, in the competitive manner of captains, was glad that I, along with Biagi, could see it. I was underdressed for the bridge, and Artie had been prepared to apologize for me, but, on the contrary, the captain said that he assumed from the fact that I was underdressed and bore the good name of his hometown in Holland, I must be a millionaire.

We docked van Slegtenhorst at the Jersey tank farm where he would deliver the rest of his oil, and tied up with half a dozen other tugs at the Moran Company boatyard on Staten Island, which is across Kill Van Kull from New Jersey. I stayed several nights on the *Christine*, and sometimes Biagi had work to do as late as midnight or as early as five in the morning, so he is not a barfly. But I went across the street to visit Frank's and Ginger's, two tugmen's hangouts that still charge only thirty cents for a glass of beer. The barmaid at Frank's was a great, husky, slam-bang young lady who sang along with the jukebox for hours, but louder, and swung her body in the go-go style with such tireless pleasure that she made the place fun for everybody else, as well as for herself, and, in the wee hours, was inclined to treat the weary souls ranged in a row in front of her as a harem.

"My man from Moran," she would say, not meaning anybody in particular, though there were strays off the street, too, pleading with her. "I'm fifty-seven years old and still making a hundred forty-three dollars a week," said the man on the stool next to me very sadly, but she was so delighted with the music, her job, and the audience, she didn't linger for long to commiserate with him.

At dawn the water was milk-colored, red "nun" buoys clanged beside the channel back to Manhattan, and burnt-yellow ferryboats were crossing from St. George to the Battery. As we hurried to meet the Dole fruit boat *Bolivar* off Governor's Island, Biagi welcomed the new day in the noisy galley with his breakfast eggs—the yolks like breasts —"Good morning, dear!"

We docked the *Bolivar* at Pier 42, on the east side of Manhattan; then the coffee freighter *Ciudad de Cucuta* across the East River at Pier 3 in Brooklyn. We sailed the *Rio Amazonas* from Pier 5, Brooklyn, and the *Rio Teuco* from Pier 2, and soon afterwards, since we were working there, docked the *Asunción*, a slender little cargo ship, at Pier 8, and sailed the car carrier *Höegh Target*, based in Oslo, from Pier 9. Before lunch, we went down the harbor to Thirty-ninth Street, Brooklyn, and sailed the *Delta American*, captained by a Southerner who said he had never been North before and was glad to be leaving.

Red Nordberg, who claimed that he was "not a moderate

drinker—what I start I finish," talked about practical jokes he had played. Nailing a mate's shoes to the floor and waking him up for midnight watch, or putting cut-up rubber bands in his pipe and a lobster in his bunk, or pulling the tug's whistle by means of a rope from another tug, if they were all tied up for the night and he had brought his girlfriend to his cabin.

Tugmen never got much "grease" in the old days, and remain just spectators to the intrigue of drug smuggling that goes on lately. But Leo and Bobby Perlitz talked about the era when whole banana stalks would be handed to them after they had docked a fruit boat, and when the coal-barge companies gave out Christmas turkeys, and a Russian ship captain, happy at arriving in this mythical hive of a capitalist port, offered his docking pilot, besides the usual gift of fur gloves, vodka, and caviar, half an hour with the ship's whore. Some of the British boats had been crewed by Pakistanis, who kept live goats and chickens tethered on the poop deck and a stew pot cooking. You would see a couple of black women sneaking up the gangplank, first thing, as they docked, to service the crew. Nowadays, too, Bobby said, you might catch sight of a limber black woman going aboard with an amused expression, but she would be in uniform, working for Customs and Immigration.

Directed by the dispatcher to go to the South Bronx for garbaging chores, we lunched on the river, our wake spreading like fish ribs behind us. Bobby called Leo "Chico" and "Pablo," to irritate him, and a new deckhand named Niels, whom we had picked up for garbage duty, "Johnny Bicycle," because he seemed so young, quick, and dippy. Niels had just quit a busboy's job at Studio 54, the nightclub for celebrities, and talked about all the celebs he could have snorted coke with. He talked about his first job on a tug, owned by another company, which he said had once been burned out and sunk in a naphtha explosion, so that its timbering was still warped from being underwater. The captain and mate had shouted at him constantly, and while he was coiling a rope on the stern a barge they were towing lurched right over the fantail and nearly cashed in his chips for him. Raw as he was, however, he was earning $200 a day from Moran, said Biagi, instead of $200 a week, as he would have on land.

Our stubby *Christine* chuffed up the East River past the United Nations building; the Shah of Iran, who was then hospitalized in New York Hospital; Mayor Ed Koch's 1801-vintage house; and South Brother Island, which is my favorite spot (or dot) in the harbor, an undisturbed minutia of wilderness with wide-spreading trees and underbrush, opposite Tiffany Street in the Bronx.

"G-man duty" pays "mud-scale" wages, higher than ordinary wages—"mud" being sewage, which, like the city's garbage, is hauled away by water. It is lazy, smelly, fly-blown work, shifting empty barges into the waterside terminals where the sanitation trucks unload, and pulling them out again after three hours when they are full. Even though we also crossed Bowery Bay to perform the same service for the Borough of Queens, we had endless lounging time, or "government time," as Biagi called it.

I have heard other tugmen describe the wet scents of the garbage barges as reminding them of sex; and they get onto the subject of the ripening widows in their neighborhoods or apartment buildings, and want to look for a pay telephone, or get up on the rail of the barge and look for skin magazines in the heap. But the smells are mostly a compen-

17

dium of America's extraordinarily sugar-rich diet, and the main action is provided by the sea gulls, which find here a sustenance substituting for the shellfish and spawning fish of primeval New Amsterdam, now so long gone.

Sparrows, starlings, and pigeons were crawling over the garbage and one odd, humpy cattle egret, which looked cold, was feasting on insects. But it was the gulls' show. They settled themselves, vain of their wingspreads, with much kvetching, creaking and croaking, keeowing and *kuk-kuk-yucca-yucca*ing, on each fresh load, when we pulled a barge out of the shed. In what ethologists call "agonistic" behavior, they flexed their wings, pointed their heads straight up and opened their bills before sidling over and pecking each other. Herring gulls, white with pinkish legs and black wingtips, were in the majority, and busiest at ripping open the plastic bags and grabbing the chitlings inside. Then perhaps they would perch on a burned mattress that protruded over the side of the barge while gobbling these tidbits down. But numbers of large all-white glaucous gulls and several huge black-backed gulls with white necks and heads, almost eagle-sized, dominated the mob. It was altogether a scene from the end of the world, and Biagi performed a species of jujitsu with the weighty barges, as the colliding currents of Long Island Sound and Hell Gate pried at them like a crowbar to wrest them out of his control.

While we were watching the gulls he spoke of a deck-hand named "Holy John," now dead, who had believed that every sea gull was a dead seaman and had got terribly angry once when Biagi shot one. Biagi was a skeptical Catholic, and knocking his cup of coffee off the window ledge by accident—"That's my Italian accent"—he asked me what I believed about life after death. I said life was a borrowed gift; life, whether human or animal, might be as temporary as so many wavelets in the ocean that quietly fall back and can't be reconstructed again, after each rise. But the ocean they were part of was life. Life was as eternal as that.

"Now, that's worth all the trouble of having you along. All the trouble of explaining everything—just to hear one new idea like that!" Biagi exclaimed enthusiastically. "Whether it makes sense or not, that's what you don't hear on a job like this, a new idea." But I had been arguing that he had had more fun driving a tug for the last thirty years than he would have piloting airliners, so I suggested that there should be plenty of new ideas out here on the water.

It was dusk; cocktail hour. At the garbage terminal in Queens the sanitation men had hosed the barges till each one looked like a vast greenish condom. But a fancy, hightailed, silvery jet came shrieking down just above our heads every minute and a half to hit the landing strip of La Guardia Airport, which was a few hundred yards away, lit like a Christmas tree. All the luxury of rushing by taxi to the midtown hotels was implied in the fanciness, luscious lights, haste—but close by was a silent stretch of horizon where the city prison on Riker's Island is.

We were contemporaries, and Biagi was saying how at our present age he wouldn't dream of shooting a gull. He'd lost his taste, too, for the violent mood of strike time on the waterfront, when young tug-union members occasionally go touring by launch with a rifle in hand. Wouldn't it be crazy to shoot somebody over a matter of a couple of extra dollars in your paycheck? He said his wife said his check was getting too big for his own good now, anyway. People had gotten beaten up, sent to the hospital, for stepping into a phone booth to call home, when some dynamite-head on the picket line suddenly suspected that they might be finks who were calling the company.

Next morning we docked the *Hellenic Explorer*, a gray-and-white containership from Piraeus, at Thirty-third Street, Brooklyn. With a big, reassuring grin, the mate nodded at Biagi, grasping his elbows, and Biagi then entrusted his life to him for a second in swinging his body over the ship's railing, while a hard current bobbed the tug and ladder underneath him. Because I'd once lived for half a year on the Aegean, that generous Greek grin somehow struck home to me as a contrast to the softer, self-absorbed grins of landlubbers like myself whom I was seeing lately.

We also docked the *Hellenic Sky*, at Fifty-seventh Street, Brooklyn, and, in the afternoon, went up Newark Bay to sail the *Toyota Maru No. 8*, which was returning to Japan to fetch more Toyotas. While we were in Port Newark, we docked the *Covadonga*, a freighter from Barcelona, as planes took off and landed just across the fence, at Newark Airport.

In the twilight we sailed the *Export Freedom* from Howland Hook in Arthur Kill, and then, off Robbins Reef, threw a line to a Liberian scrap-metal ship and took it up Kill Van Kull, under Bayonne Bridge, around Bergen Point, and up Newark Bay to Pier 36, in Port Newark again. We sailed the *Atlantic Song*, a Swedish containership carrying backhoes and tractors, from Port Elizabeth, New Jersey, and docked the gray-and-white *Good Master*, a Greek freighter, in Brooklyn, an hour later—the Lower

Manhattan skyscrapers taking on a cathedral shape in the distance in the meantime. We docked Dow Chemical's *Leland I. Doan* in Kill Van Kull, at flood tide, and the white, trim, high-riding 697-foot South African *Alphen*, in Brooklyn, and sailed the blue 425-foot *Stubbenhuk* from Bay Ridge, Brooklyn, heading for Hamburg.

Biagi said that except for purposes of calculation, he tries to ignore how lengthy some of his ships are, in order not to become intimidated, and that he blocks out of his mind past near collisions and lesser calamities, of which a considerable number are inevitable in a lifetime of harbor work. Like a dancing elephant, a ship being docked turns slowly but gracefully and importantly in the rush of the tide in front of a row of finger piers. It will swing left or right according to which way the water is running and whether the pilot means for it to enter the slip bow-first or stern-first. But the key decision the pilot must make is when he should start the turn. Then, by watching a single landmark on shore, he estimates, adjusts and coordinates with his tugboats the ship's speed and position as it slides through what may be a 90-degree shift. The new containerships come equipped with bow thrusters and stern thrusters—extra propellers that, in effect, enable them to move sideways at will. This invention, employed in concert with the ship's main screw, could even eliminate tugs from the docking process eventually, though they would still be needed for risky passages in a tight, intricate harbor like New York's.

We had one nervous moment. At night, in the confined area between Staten Island and New Jersey, Biagi, on the bridge of the *Leland I. Doan*, seemed to lose control for a spell. The *Doan*, a tanker loaded with God knows what combination of chemicals, yawed around in a four-knot tide as if to block the channel and drift down upon a containership waiting for clearance under a railroad bridge that crossed Kill Van Kull. The *Christine* alone was not strong enough to stop her, and Biagi had not asked for a backup tug to help. Finally, he saved the situation by first cutting and then after a moment starting the ship's own engines, while the captain of the *Doan*, standing beside him, clutched the edge of a table until his knuckles turned white.

Afterwards, in the *Christine*'s galley, Bobby, to relieve the tension, said a tug captain "must have big balls. That's half the job." He teased Decker, the engineer or "Chief," with Indian-chief jokes; said "How" to him. Decker, for his part, teased Biagi about being "only a pointer." The engine was the center of a boat, Decker said—even the old *Christine*'s had once made a trip clear to Vietnam—and the captain "only points where it should go."

Tugboatmen, although they have seamen's papers, quickly shrug off their allegiance to ships and the sea after each job. More than taxi drivers, they are really citizens of the city. They barge the sand the buildings are built of down the Hudson from Haverstraw, and get their water from Pier 36 in Brooklyn's Gowanus Bay. They can tie up anywhere, in any borough, for a catnap, and up the street there is a bar and a betting parlor. "Up the street" in waterside Brooklyn, Manhattan, Long Island City, Hoboken, and Weehawken was where all the nightlife was; and in such an enormous dukedom, if a tugman got into trouble in one neck of the harbor, he could do his drinking in another —or just cross the river. If he had a goon squad chasing him, he ran straight for the water, tiptoed down the stringpiece of the wharf, hopped onto his boat, and confidently threw the engine into full reverse—out into the sprawling harbor, simmering with lights at night.

Years ago, a tugman was likely to stay with the same boat until at last he was carried off feetfirst. And so, once somebody had learned the shapes of the different vessels in the Moran fleet and knew the patterns of their running lights, he could look around the Upper Bay and see where his friends were working, even at night.

1979

WHAT I THINK,
WHAT I AM

Our loneliness makes us avoid
column readers these days. The personalities in the San
Francisco *Chronicle*, Chicago *Daily News*, New York *Post*
constitute our neighbors now, some of them local characters but also the opinionated national stars. And movie re-
viewers thrive on our yearning for somebody emotional
who is willing to pay attention to us and return week after
week, year after year, through all the to-and-fro of other
friends, to flatter us by pouring out his/her heart. They
are essayists of a type, as Elizabeth Hardwick is, James
Baldwin was.

We sometimes hear that essays are an old-fashioned form,
that so-and-so is the "last essayist," but the facts of the marketplace argue quite otherwise. Essays of nearly any kind
are so much easier than short stories for a writer to sell, so
many more see print, it's strange that though two fine an-
thologies remain that publish the year's best stories, no

comparable collection exists for essays. Such changes in the reading public's taste aren't always to the good, needless to say. The art of telling stories predated even cave painting, surely; and if we ever find ourselves living in caves again, it (with painting and drumming) will be the only art left, after movies, novels, photography, essays, biography, and all the rest have gone down the drain—the art to build from.

One has the sense with the short story as a form that while everything may have been done, nothing has been overdone; it has a permanence. Essays, if a comparison is to be made, although they go back four hundred years to Montaigne, seem a mercurial, newfangled, sometimes hokey affair that has lent itself to many of the excesses of the age, from spurious autobiography to spurious hallucination, as well as to the shabby careerism of traditional journalism. It's a greased pig. Essays are associated with the way young writers fashion a name—on plain, crowded newsprint in hybrid vehicles like the *Village Voice*, *Rolling Stone*, the *New York Review of Books*, instead of the thick paper stock and thin readership of *Partisan Review*.

Essays, however, hang somewhere on a line between two sturdy poles: this is what I think, and this is what I am. Autobiographies which aren't novels are generally extended essays, indeed. A personal essay is like the human voice talking, its order the mind's natural flow, instead of a systematized outline of ideas. Though more wayward or informal than an article or treatise, somewhere it contains a point which is its real center, even if the point couldn't be uttered in fewer words than the essayist has used. Essays don't usually boil down to a summary, as articles do, and the style of the writer has a "nap" to it, a combination of personality and originality and energetic loose ends that stand up like the nap on a piece of wool and can't be brushed flat. Essays belong to the animal kingdom, with a surface that generates sparks, like a coat of fur, compared with the flat, conventional cotton of the magazine article writer, who works in the vegetable kingdom, instead. But essays, on the other hand, may have fewer "levels" than fiction, because we are not supposed to argue much about their meaning. In the old distinction between teaching and storytelling, the essayist, however cleverly he camouflages his intentions, is a bit of a teacher or reformer, and an essay is intended to convey the same point to each of us.

This emphasis upon mind speaking to mind is what makes essays less universal in their appeal than stories. They are addressed to an educated, perhaps a middle-class, reader, with certain presuppositions, a frame of reference, even a commitment to civility that is shared—not the grand and golden empathy inherent in every man or woman that a storyteller has a chance to tap.

Nevertheless, the artful "I" of an essay can be as chameleon as any narrator in fiction; and essays do tell a story quite as often as a short story stakes a claim to a particular viewpoint. Mark Twain's piece called "Corn-pone Opinions," for example, which is about public opinion, begins with a vignette as vivid as any in *Huckleberry Finn*. Twain says that when he was a boy of fifteen, he used to hang out a back window and listen to the sermons preached by a neighbor's slave standing on top of a woodpile: "He imitated the pulpit style of the several clergymen of the village, and did it well and with fine passion and energy. To me he was a wonder. I believed he was the greatest orator in the United States and would some day be heard from. But it did not happen; in the distribution of rewards he was overlooked. . . . He interrupted his preaching now and then

26

to saw a stick of wood, but the sawing was a pretense—he did it with his mouth, exactly imitiating the sound the bucksaw makes in shrieking its way through the wood. But it served its purpose, it kept his master from coming out to see how the work was getting along."

A novel would go on and tell us what happened next in the life of the slave—and we miss that. But the extraordinary flexibility of essays is what has enabled them to ride out rough weather and hybridize into forms that suit the times. And just as one of the first things a fiction writer learns is that he needn't actually be writing fiction to write a short story—that he can tell his own history or anybody else's as exactly as he remembers it and it will be "fiction" if it remains primarily a story—an essayist soon discovers that he doesn't have to tell the whole truth and nothing but the truth; he can shape or shave his memories, as long as the purpose is served of elucidating a truthful point. A personal essay frequently is not autobiographical at all, but what it does keep in common with autobiography is that, through its tone and tumbling progression, it conveys the quality of the author's mind. Nothing gets in the way. Because essays are directly concerned with the mind and the mind's idiosyncrasy, the very freedom the mind possesses is bestowed on this branch of literature that does honor to it, and the fascination of the mind is the fascination of the essay.

1976

MUSHPAN
MAN

There is in the western country a very extraordinary missionary of the New Jerusalem. A man has appeared who seems to be almost independent of corporal wants and sufferings. He goes barefooted, can sleep anywhere, in house or out of house, and live upon the coarsest and most scanty fare. He has actually thawed the ice with his bare feet.

He procures what books he can of the New Church; travels into the remote settlements, and lends them wherever he can find readers, and sometimes divides a book into two or three parts for more extensive distribution and usefulness.

This man for years past has been in the employment of bringing into cultivation, in numberless places in the wilderness, small patches (two or three acres) of ground, and then sowing apple seeds and rearing nurseries. . . .

—From a report of the
*Society for Printing, Publishing and Circulating
the Writings of Emanuel Swedenborg,*
Manchester, England, January 1817

. . . he ran with the rabbit and slept with the stream."

—Vachel Lindsay,
In Praise of Johnny Appleseed

Of Jonathan Chapman
Two things are known,
That he loved apples,
That he walked Alone. . . .

The Stalking Indian,
The beast in its lair
Did no hurt
While he was there.

For they could tell,
As wild things can,
That Jonathan Chapman
Was God's own man.

—From *A Book of Americans*,
by Rosemary and Stephen Vincent Benét

He was real flesh and blood, not a folk construction like Paul Bunyan—and he plied the trade of an appleman for almost fifty years with inspired generosity, not ascending solely to a single day's public drama, like John Henry, the steel-driving hero of Big Bend Tunnel in West Virginia. Yet Johnny Appleseed, too, has survived simply as a folk figure of whom little is known, as a memory fuzzy in outline, mainly inscribed in children's literature and turn-of-the-century romances and poetry or Louis Bromfield novels.

Born John Chapman (1774–1845) in Leominster, Massachusetts, he proved to be a man with a mission along the frontier, which in those days included western Pennsylvania, Ohio, Indiana, and Illinois. If he had kept a diary, he might be compared with John James Audubon and George Catlin, who come down to us through their own words and pictures, although—more of a frontiersman than they were—he worked humbly and busily to facilitate that frontier's passing. In a way, his name is as durable as Andrew Jackson's, who died in the same year. But he has been remarkably neglected by the historians, probably because he conforms to none of the national stereotypes and illustrates nobody's theories.

We think of the swaggering, unscrupulous prototype frontiersman who bushwhacked Indians and scouted for the Long Knives, the mountainman who went into the bush with two horses and a squaw, and in order to live, ate his packhorse in January, his saddle horse in February, and his sad squaw in March. In the gaudy parade of liars, killers, pranksters, boasters, and boosters that fill up B. A. Botkin's *A Treasury of American Folklore*, Johnny Appleseed, along with Abe Lincoln and George Washington, occupies a tiny section entitled "Patron Saints." (John Henry and Paul Bunyan are "Miracle Men.") But, though a legendary walker, he is fabled as much for abusing his feet as for sporting tin pots on his head or cardboard headgear. In icy weather, at best he wore castoffs given to him—sometimes one shoe and one broken boot, tied on with varicolored string wound around his ankle, sometimes only one shoe, with which he broke trail through the snow for his bare foot. He preferred, if possible, nothing at all. There is the story of Johnny quietly confronting a pharisaical camp-meeting preacher who had demanded of the congregation, "Where now is the man like the primitive Christian who is traveling to Heaven barefooted and clad in coarse raiment?" Johnny, of course, walked forward in the upside-down coffee sack with holes for his head and arms that was his usual garb, and lifted his bruised bare feet, one by one, putting them right on the pulpit stump.

Nowadays we like heroes in *boots*, however. Saxophone players, clerical workers, hair stylists, "anti-heroes," ladies dressed for the office, partially disrobed ladies, vacationers fussily dashing into an airport taxi, all are likely to wear cowboy boots, jackboots, ski boots, sandhog boots, desert boots, with kinky belt buckles that broadcast a physical vigor and spiritual sadism the wearer doesn't really even aspire to feel. Our great West, our old westering impulse, has become a costume jewel.

Anomalous, unassimilable, Johnny Appleseed was a frontiersman who would not eat meat, who wished not to kill so much as a rattlesnake, who pitied the very mosquitoes that flew into the smoke of his campfire. He liked to hear the wolves howl around him at night and was unafraid of bears, yet reportedly slept without shelter one snowy night rather than roust out of hibernation a mother bear and her cubs who had crept into a hollow tree that he had intended using. Although he would sometimes buy a worn-out horse to save it from mistreatment, boarding it with one of his friends for the winter, and would scour the woods in the fall for lame horses that the pioneers, packing their way through the country, had abandoned, apparently he believed that riding the beasts was discourteous to them. He only employed a horse to carry his bags of seeds or, late in his life, to drag an old wagon.

Though in a sense he was the nation's paramount nineteenth-century orchardist, Johnny Appleseed denounced as wickedness the practices of grafting and pruning, by which all commercial fruit is produced, because of the torture he thought such a knifing must inflict on the tree. He was shy in a crowd but a regular sermonizer among people he felt at home with—probably a bit of a bore at times, but no simpleton. In Steubenville, Cincinnati, and Urbana, Ohio, he knew the leading New Church Swedenborgians, and between his arrival in central and northern Ohio and the time of his death, Swedenborgian societies sprang up in at least twelve of the counties there, many individuals testifying that it was Chapman, the colporteur of Christian literature, who had first "planted the seed."

As a religious enthusiast, he was more on the Franciscan model than the harsh zealots, from Puritan to Mormon, whom American social historians are accustomed to writing about. And as an entrepreneur with considerable foresight about the eventual patterns of settlement, he allowed himself to be utterly clipped and gypped in matters of real estate through much of his life. When somebody jumped one of his land claims, his main concern seemed to be whether they would still let him take care of his apple trees. When he sold apple seedlings, he liked to be paid with an IOU, scarcely having any use for money except to give it away to needy families, and left to God and the debtor's own conscience the question of whether he was finally paid. Instead, he bartered for potatoes, cornmeal, salt, and flour, and peddled cranberries—a fruit that the pioneers combined into stews or dried with suet for a midwinter treat. Often he shucked corn, split rails, and girdled trees for his keep. He ate nuts and wild plums in the woods on his trips, and cooked his corn mush, roasted his potatoes, and probably carried Indian-style "journey bread," which was made by boiling green corn till it was half done, drying it again in the sun, then browning it in hot ashes when ready to eat, pounding it fine, and possibly stirring in birch or maple syrup or summer berries or honey (though Johnny always left enough of that in the comb for the bees to live on). If many people never paid him for the seedlings he distributed so diligently, others returned his kindness by their hospitality to him as he passed back and forth. The belt of territory he worked in shifted gradually westward during the course of his life, but he wintered in the easternmost towns—after his strenuous summers at the borders of settlement—and so would migrate between several homesites, several circles of friends.

He gave little gifts of tea when he had money, but probably didn't drink it himself, preferring a Biblical drink of milk or milk and honey. He did use snuff, however, and would sip a dram of hard liquor to warm up in cold weather—if one can generalize fairly about his conduct from isolated instances of testimony about five decades of such intense and fervent activity. He was wiry in build, short by our standards but average for then, with peculiarly piercing blue eyes, good teeth, a scanty dark beard that later turned gray, and uncut dark hair, parted down the middle and tucked behind his ears. When not in a coffee sack, he dressed in a collarless tow-linen smock or straight-sleeved coat that hung down to his heels, over a shirt and burr-studded pants that had been traded to him for his apple seeds.

He was quick-talking and restlessly energetic as a visitor, but wind-beaten, hollow-cheeked, and gaunt-looking from eating so little and walking so far. Yet somehow, despite his eccentric demeanor, he was remarkably effective in the impression he made, "some rare force of gentle goodness dwelling in his looks and breathing in his words," as W. D. Haley wrote in *Harper's New Monthly Magazine* for November 1871, in the first biographical sketch that brought Johnny Appleseed to national attention. Not even small boys made fun of him, knowing his boldness at bearing pain —besides walking barefoot in the snow, he would poke needles into himself without flinching, for the children's edification. He had a string of good stories of Indians and wolves for them, and presents of ribbon and whatnot that he carried with him to give to their sisters.

He felt comfortable with children, and probably wistful, particularly with girls. Holding a six-year-old child on his lap, he would speak of someday having a "pure wife in Heaven." He seems to have imagined that it might be possible to adopt an orphan of about that age and raise her up to be just such a wife, even on earth. There are indications that at least once he tried, but that in adolescence the girl, like other girls, began to flirt with other men. Another time he announced that two female spirits had shown themselves to him and told him they would be his wives in the afterlife, bidding him abstain until then. He took an untheatrical view of the hereafter, however—a place he didn't think would be all that different in geography or its earthly occupations from the world he lived in. Resurrection was the simple continuation of the spiritual being without its corporeal, or "natural," adjuncts, and the indifference to physical discomfort which he cultivated can no doubt be partly ascribed to his impatience to see that process speeded, says Robert Price, his principal biographer. But he liked to joke that Hades at its worst wouldn't be worse than "smoky houses and scolding women" or "Newark," a raunchy Ohio border settlement.

Despite his small roach of a beard, unkemptly clipped, and his dark horny feet and deliberately apostolic costume, he kept himself clean, and "in his most desolate rags" was "never repulsive," his acquaintances reported. Arriving at a house where he was known, he happily stretched out on his back on the floor near the door, with his head on his knapsack and his feet tilted up against the log wall. Removing his discolored Bible and Swedenborgian tracts from the pouch he created for them inside his smock by tying his belt tightly, he would ask with exuberance, "Will you have some fresh news right from Heaven?" While the men smoked or fleshed a fox skin and the women cooked or quilted, he read and extemporized, his voice now roaring scriptural denunciations of evil, now soft and soothing. By middle age, he didn't hesitate to introduce himself to strangers as "Johnny Appleseed," enjoying his notoriety, but before accepting hospitality he would make sure there was plenty of food in the house for the children.

In good weather he slept outside; otherwise he would lie down on the floor close to the door of the cabin, as he "did not expect to sleep in a bed in the next world." But one can picture the suppers of applesauce, apple pie, apple strudel, apple dumplings, apple turnover, apple cider, apple butter, and apple brown betty he was served by farm wives who had settled in the vicinity of his nurseries. One also can imagine the kidding he endured for bringing hard cider and applejack into the country (which already had "white lightning"—corn liquor). After the article in *Harper's* by W. D. Haley, twenty-six years after his death, there was a sudden revival of interest in Johnny Appleseed, with people writing their recollections or hearsay memories of him to small-town newspapers throughout the Midwest. He was compared to John the Baptist, a voice in the wilderness heralding a new religion, and professors said he had personified the spirit of democracy—one for all—in the New World. In more saccharine accounts, professional romancers reported that apple blossoms tapped at his window when he was born and strewed themselves over his grave when he died. "His mush-pan slapped on his windy head, his torn shirt flapping, his eyes alight, an American ghost," wrote Frances Frost.

"In his earthly life," Ophia D. Smith noted in a centennial tribute by Swedenborgians in 1945, "Johnny Appleseed was a one-man circulating library, a one-man humane society, a one-man [medical] clinic, a one-man missionary band, and a one-man emigrant-aid society." But because of the distance that separates us, and as a result of the void in scholarship until Robert Price's biography in 1954—the fact that for many years historians simply ignored him as a character fit only for children's stories—we can't make a good estimate of the quality of his mind. We do know he corresponded with a distinguished coreligionist in Philadelphia, William Schlatter, who was also his supplier of evangelical tracts, though, unfortunately, none of Chapman's letters have survived. We know, too, that he planted medicinal herbs wherever he went, plants such as mullein, pennyroyal, catnip, horehound, rattlesnake root, wintergreen, and dandelion (a native of Europe), instructing the settlers in their use. His favorite was the two-foot-high, bad-smelling mayweed, or "dogfennel," another alien, which spoiled the taste of milk when cows ate it and for a while was called "johnnyweed," with the idea that he might have been planting it everywhere as a practical joke. On the contrary, he seems to have really believed that its noxious smell in every Ohio dooryard would ward off outbreaks of malaria.

We know that he stayed out of fights in the rowdiest communities, even when provoked, according to his adage of living by the law of love although fearing no man. But we don't know how consistently he refused to eat animal flesh, or how constantly cheerful he was, or whether his habits of self-punishment—which smack of the perverse to our modern temperament—discomposed his neighbors, who were an infinitely hardier lot and more inclined to defer to the example of the self-mortifying earlier Christian martyrs. Though he must have brewed gentler poultices for other people's wounds, his method of healing his own was to sear the offending location with a hot piece of iron—as the Indians did—and then treat the burn. Such fortitude won the Indians' respect, and he planted some trees in the Indian villages as well as in white towns. For his stoicism, his knowledge of herbal medicine, and his selflessness, which they recognized as a manifestation of godliness, they seem to have revered him. More important, he respected and sympathized with them at a time when many white woodsmen shot them on sight like vermin, to clear the woods, or else humiliated them by catching their horses and tying sticks in their mouths and clapboards to their tails and letting the horses run home with the clapboards on fire. Swedenborg himself had said, "All things in the world exist from a Divine Origin . . . clothed with such forms in nature as enable them to exist here and perform their use and thus correspond to higher things." So the Swedenborgian spirit-world of souls and angels coexistent with a natural world, in which the true order of Creation had been diverted by man's misapplication of his free will from the love of God to his own ego, quite corresponded, as far as it went, with the Indians' view. To his credit, Chapman, who seems to have been friendly with the Quakers of Ohio, too, was able to recognize this.

He was born—John Chapman—in poor circumstances in Leominster, in a cabin overlooking the Nashua River. His father, Nathaniel, was a farmer, carpenter, and wheelwright descended from Edward Chapman, who had arrived in Boston from Shropshire in 1639. Scarcely a year after the birth of John, his second child, the father left to fight in the Revolution as one of the original minutemen, first at Bunker Hill in 1775, then with George Washington's army in New York the next year, wintering at Valley Forge in 1777–78. John's mother had died, meanwhile. In 1780, following his discharge as a captain, Nathaniel Chapman married again, a Miss Lucy Cooley of Longmeadow, near Springfield, Massachusetts, and fathered ten more children by her. Though we have no proof that "Johnny Appleseed" was brought from his grandparents' house in Leominster to grow up here, he probably did spend his later boyhood on the Connecticut River, learning to handle a raft and pirogue, learning about wildlife, with this new brood.

Longmeadow was on the Connecticut Path, walked by settlers going west toward the upper Susquehanna River, two hundred miles away. It's thought that John Chapman, around 1792, at the age of eighteen, set out with his half brother Nathaniel, who was seven years younger, for this frontier. They paused in the Wilkes-Barre region for a year or two, then may have ventured south to the Potomac in eastern Virginia and dawdled along from there toward Fort Cumberland, and then, via Braddock's Road, to the Monongahela, and on by 1797 to Pittsburgh, during what was now John Adams's presidency. According to one story, they traveled up the Allegheny that fall to Olean, New York, in search of an uncle who was supposed to have built a cabin there, only to discover that he had pushed on west. With scant provisions, they took over his abandoned home, and nearly starved. What saved them, it's said, is that while John hiked out to earn money for food, some passing Indians luckily dropped in on his brother and provisioned him and taught him to hunt. (We don't know if John was already a vegetarian—which would have been a terrible disadvantage for both in enduring such a winter.)

In any case, the experience may have estranged the two. With the warm weather, they separated—Nathaniel, in his late teens, being old enough to strike off independently and to settle eventually on Duck Creek near Marietta in southern Ohio on the Ohio River, where by 1805 Nathaniel, Sr., the former minuteman, also moved with his family. The older Chapman, though a captain in time of war, had been an indifferent provider, and died in 1807. One of his daughters, named Persis, and nineteen years younger than Johnny Appleseed, later was to play an important and softening role in Johnny's life; but there is little evidence that John and Nathaniel ever troubled to see much of each other again, until 1842. That was fifty years after they had sauntered out from Longmeadow together, and John, famous and cranky and old, with a "thick bark of queerness on him," as Robert Price expresses it, and only three years short of his death, trudged east from Fort Wayne, Indiana, where he was living with Persis and her family, to Marietta, for a final reunion.

Mr. Price—who devoted, he says, the better part of twenty-five years to sifting the provable from unprovable legends about Johnny Appleseed—does not believe that the Chapman boys ever went from Wilkes-Barre to Virginia. Indeed, with the affectionate overfamiliarity of an expert who has perhaps overmastered a subject, he slightly belittles the legends he does believe. But he ascribes adventures aplenty to them in the area of the upper Allegheny near Warren, in northwestern Pennsylvania, where he has found evidence that they had moved in 1797. In the spring of 1798, along Big Brokenstraw Creek, Johnny may have planted his first apple seeds. Only four other settlers were in residence on the creek, but they were busy fellows who within ten years would be rafting pine logs clear to New Orleans. Johnny probably lost his patches of orchard land to a more aggressive citizen. The next season—his brother gone by now—he had moved fifty miles, to French Creek, another tributary of the Allegheny. He was exceedingly vigorous, doubtless a whiz at wielding an ax (one posthumous legend has him competing with Paul Bunyan). This was a time of wrestling great oaks and stupendous pines, of big snowstorms, when reportedly he toughed out one winter holed up on an island on French Creek subsisting on butternuts alone. That spring, or another, he was so impatient to get an early start downriver that he set his canoe on a block of ice on the Allegheny, where it would not be crushed in the jams, and fell asleep and floated a hundred miles or so before he bothered to wake up.

It was an element in the myth of Johnny Appleseed that he could doze off in the most dangerous circumstances—so calm he was. Once, in Seneca territory, he was being chased by a war party, before he had made his name favorably known to the tribe, and as the story goes, he slipped into a swampy reedbed and lay with just his mouth above water, napping until the warriors gave up hunting him. In Ohio the Indians he knew were Delawares, Mohicans, and Wyandots, who were soon driven out of the state in the aftermath of the attacks they mounted (or allegedly hoped to mount) with British encouragement during the War of 1812. That summer and fall, with his woodcraft and marathon-endurance, John Chapman fulfilled a hero's role, once racing thirty miles from Mansfield to Mount Vernon, Ohio, to summon reinforcements and arouse the white settlers to the peril posed by General William Hull's surrender to British forces at Detroit. He spouted Biblical language, according to at least one witness, and inevitably there were some false alarms: "The spirit of the Lord is upon me, and he hath anointed me to blow the trumpet in the wilderness, and sound an alarm in the forest; for behold, the tribes of the heathen are round about your doors, and a devouring flame followeth after them." This is the self-dramatist in him that made Casey Jones, John Henry, and Davy Crockett heroes also.

Casey Jones died from driving his locomotive faster than he ought to have. But Mr. Price reminds us that Chapman lived out his three score and ten years, and that the error of folklore is to simplify. The young buck strenuously logging, snowshoeing, existing on butternuts in the French Creek period, must have been quite a different figure from

"Johnny Appleseed" practicing his kindnesses and charities during the two and a half decades when he lived in Ohio and brought apples to Ashland, Bucyrus, Cohocton, Findlay, New Haven, Van Wert, and many another town on giveaway terms. Odd as he was—with the gossip that trailed him hinting that earlier in life he may have been kicked in the head by a horse—he almost seems to have passed for a solid citizen here. People didn't mind him dandling their babies. He even suffered (we may infer) the very insignia of solid citizenship, a "mid-life crisis," somewhere during the years from 1809 to 1824, when he would have been between thirty-five and fifty years old.

That is, he had been a mystic before, and he ended his days in Indiana as a kind of landmark, with the "thick bark of queerness" still on him, thoroughly a mystic again. But for a few years in central Ohio, apparently he tried to become a practical man. He speculated in a couple of town lots in Mount Vernon, one of which he sold after nineteen years for a profit of five dollars. By 1815 he had leased four quarter sections of land of a hundred and sixty acres each for ninety-nine years at nineteen dollars a year apiece—a Mrs. Jane Cunningham his partner. But a recession occurred in 1819, tightening the money supply miserably. As a man accustomed to selling his goods for IOU's, he saw his principal holdings forfeited for want of money. His biographer makes the point that toward the close of his life, perhaps under Persis's influence, he bought another two hundred acres, around Fort Wayne. Altogether, a documented total of twenty-two properties, amounting to twelve hundred acres, can be totted up that he leased or owned for a time. But it would be a good guess to say that he accepted the 1819 recession as a lesson that he was intended to be an appleman, not a speculator, and an instrument of the bounty of God.

He had arrived on the Licking River in Ohio from the Allegheny in 1801, aged twenty-six. Only three families lived in what has become Licking County, but Ohio was just two years short of statehood by then. Ebenezer Zane was blazing Zane's Trace from Wheeling, on the Ohio River, through Zanesville and Chillicothe, capital of the Northwest Territory, toward Maysville, Kentucky. Farther north, there was an access path from Pittsburgh for a hundred and sixty miles to the Black Fork of the Mohican River, and from Pittsburgh by an old Indian trail to Fort Sandusky and on toward Detroit.

He seems to have come this first time on foot with a horseload of seeds. More than three hundred thousand apple seeds will fit in a single bushel, so he had his work cut out for him. He may have been wearing his fabled mushpan on his head (if he ever did), with plenty of plantings in Pennsylvania behind him, and his vision of the figure he wanted to cut for the rest of his life in front of him. But we don't know if Johnny preferred winter to summer apples, or sharp flavors to sweet. We don't really know how hard he worked, because, set against this picture of a religious zealot, for whom apple trees in their flowering were a living sermon from God, is the carefree master of woodcraft who supposedly strung his hammock between treetops and lazed away the pleasant days.

He came back in succeeding summers to his nurseries to tend them—back to these patent and bounty lands "homesteaded," in a later phrase, or deeded to Revolutionary soldiers, or to the Refugee Tract, which was reserved for Canadians who had been persecuted by the British, or the

Firelands, granted to Connecticut citizens in recompense for damage inflicted during the war. Straight land sales on settled portions of the Ohio River at this time involved terms of two dollars an acre, with fifty cents down.

In 1806—and perhaps the prettiest of all of the memories of John Chapman that have survived—he was noticed by a settler in Jefferson County, on the Ohio, drifting past in two canoes lashed together and heaped with cider-press seeds, both craft being daubed with mud and draped with moss to keep the load moist. He stopped to establish a planting a couple of miles below town, and probably another at the mouth of the Muskingum, at Marietta, near where his father had settled the year before. Ascending the Muskingum, past Zanesville, to a tributary called Walhonding, or White Woman's Creek, where the Licking River comes in, he poled up to the Mohican River and finally to the Black Fork of the Mohican, where he already may have had a nursery growing, because central Ohio by now was not unfamiliar country to him. His earlier seedlings would have been ready to sell if five years had passed.

With this canoe trip, apparently, his fame began. He had been a local character, but there were other applemen who made a business of selling trees, mostly as a sideline to farming. (Five pennies per sapling was the price at the time.) Furthermore, a hundred years before John Chapman ever arrived, the French had brought apple seeds to the Great Lakes and Mississippi, so that some of the Indian towns along the old trails already had orchards, from which the settlers could trade or pilfer as the Indians were gradually driven away. Where Johnny differed was that he alone had set himself the task of anticipating the patterns of settlement, as a public mission, across what had become by 1803 the State of Ohio. He moved along coincident with or a step ahead of the first flying parties of settlers, to have apple trees of transplantable age ready for them when they got their land cleared. Apple vinegar was the basic preservative for pickling vegetables such as beans, cucumbers, and beets; apple butter was a principal pleasure of winter meals; and apple brandy was one of the first cash exports that could be floated downriver to New Orleans. So he began to be recognized as something of a public servant as he went about.

He planted on loamy, grassy ground, usually at riverside, constructing a fence of the brush and trees that he had cut down, and girdling any bigger trees that stood near enough to cast their shade over the soil. He would clear a patch and plant and fence it, sometimes sleeping in his hammock—looking startlingly serene, swinging there, to travelers who were full of frightening tales of the woods. Or he might strip slabs of bark from a giant elm, and lay them against it for a lean-to, or toss together a quick Indian hut of poles and bark, stretching out on a bed of leaves inside. And then he drifted on, grubbed more ground clear, constructed another barrier fence. Some of these little gardens he never bothered to hunt up again, confident that the settlers would discover them. Others he hurried back to, hearing that a herd of cattle had broken in. Hogs ranged through these oak, hickory, and beech forests, as well as cattle, and there were great flocks of passenger pigeons, and wolves, which the more brutal pioneers skinned alive and turned loose to scare the rest of the pack. On the Whetstone River, near the Clear Fork of the Mohican, the Vandorn boys helped him to build a fourteen-by-sixteen-foot cabin for wintering over, impressed at how fearlessly he slept on top of a windfall as the wolves and owls howled.

He liked to plant on quarter sections set aside for the support of the first schools, or he might do so on an existing farm if the owner agreed to share what grew. Once a few years had passed, he wouldn't need to make such long trips for seeds and, if he was then working thirty miles away, might deputize a farmer who lived close to an orchard to honor the notes he wrote out for people who wished to purchase trees.

By 1816 Persis had moved with her family from Marietta to Perrysville, Ohio, on the Mohican's Black Fork. Mansfield lay between the Clear and Black forks, and Mount Vernon was on the Kokosing, which wasn't far off. So, with some of his kin in the area (his brother-in-law worked for him), and with the goodwill that his exploits in the War of 1812 had engendered, and the investments in land that he was attempting to pay for, the region around Perrysville became his home. During his forties he traveled less, but even after he had lost most of his land and had renewed his vows of poverty—moving west again with horse-loads of apple seeds to the Miami and Tiffin rivers—he came back to Perrysville to winter with family and friends.

His fifties seem to have been severely austere, like his twenties and thirties. He planted on the Sandusky; had fifteen thousand trees at Milan on the Huron; started a nursery in Defiance in northwest Ohio when that village was six years old, and other nurseries along the proposed route of the Miami and Erie Canal. From Toledo he traveled west up the Maumee River toward Indiana, working the banks of its tributaries—the Blanchard, the Auglaize, the St. Mary's—the population of Ohio, meanwhile, having vaulted from 45,000 in 1800 to 580,00 in 1820.

In 1822 he may have gone to Detroit to sightsee, and, around 1826, to Urbana and Cincinnati. In 1830, just after the future city of Fort Wayne had been platted, he is said to have landed on the waterside from the Maumee in a hol-

46

low log filled with seeds. Thereafter he labored in Indiana, boarding with Allen County families like the Hills and Worths for a dollar or two per week, but still going back to Perrysville to spend each winter, until 1834, when Persis and her husband moved out to join him.

Various myths have him continuing on to the Ozarks, to Minnesota, to the foothills of the Rockies. He did not, but undoubtedly he gave seeds to pioneers who ventured much farther west. He may have seen Illinois and the Mississippi River and crossed into Iowa. But Allen County lies at the watershed separating the Wabash, flowing to the Mississippi, from the Maumee, flowing toward Lake Erie and eventually the St. Lawrence River, so it is appropriate that Johnny stopped here. Like the plainsmen and mountainmen, he was a man still "with the bark on," but apples were his particular witness to God, and apples do not grow well on the Great Plains. "I, John Chapman (by occupation a gatherer and planter of apple seeds)," begins a deed from the Fort Wayne days. He was an appleman first of all. Maybe he didn't even long to participate in the drama of the Great West ahead.

He was a legend by now—a bluebird to the bluejay figure of the raftsman Mike Fink, who had poled the Ohio River nearby at about the same time. Mike Fink, a very rough guy who died twenty years earlier than Johnny on a trip to the Rockies, once set his common-law wife on fire in a pyre of leaves when she winked at another man. He is more typical of the frontiersmen we remember. What would a conventional moviemaker do with a vegetarian frontiersman like Johnny who did not believe in horseback riding and wore no furs; who planted fruit trees in praise of a Protestant God, and gave much of his money away to impoverished families he met; who would "punish" one foot that had stepped on an angleworm by walking with it bare over stony ground; who would douse his campfire when mosquitoes fell into it, and regretted for years killing a rattlesnake that had bitten him in the grass?

Near Persis's home in Fort Wayne, he had a log cabin and eleven cleared acres and timber cut for a barn when he died in 1845. He died not there but at the home of the Worth family on the St. Joseph River not far off, presumably of pneumonia contracted during a fifteen-mile trudge in mid-March, leading his black ox, to repair an orchard fence that cattle had trampled down. At his death—so the Worths said—he had on a coffee sack, as well as the waist sections of four pairs of old pants, cut off and slit so that they lapped "like shingles" around his hips, under an antiquated pair of pantaloons. His life had extended from the battle of Bunker Hill to the inauguration of James K. Polk as President; and the last person who claimed to have seen Johnny Appleseed with his own eyes didn't die until just before World War II.

As that 1871 issue of *Harper's* expressed it, he was a frontier hero "of endurance that was voluntary, and of action that was creative and not sanguinary." Perhaps it is inevitable that our memory of history should become oversimplified, but lately the distortion always seems to err on the side of violence. Anyone who examines the pioneering period will find that there were a good many selfless, gentle characters who belie the violent-entrepreneurial caricatures. Historians, by neglecting individuals of such munificent spirit as Johnny, and leaving us with only the braggarts and killers, underestimate the breadth of frontier experience, and leave us the poorer.

1979

MOUNTAIN NOTCH

The little mountain in the Northeast Highlands of Vermont where I live is a knoll of low-grade granite and occasional schist more than three hundred million years old. One can date its origins, therefore, to about the time amphibians emerged on earth, and to the age of ferns. It stretches from west to east in the shape of a whale, with stunted spruces clinging in clefts of bare rock on the very top, and chatter marks gouged on the surface by the sole of the last glacier that worked it over, about twenty thousand years ago. At the whale's forehead are free-fall cliffs four hundred feet tall, so that, from a certain angle at a certain hour, at a distance of three miles, the mountain looks like a wave of breaking surf facing the rising sun. But on foggy mornings the clouds hide these dimensions and contours, making the mountain bulk bigger (if I want it to be bigger) than it really is.

A pair of bobcats generally dens in the jumbled boulders

around the bottom of the cliffs. I encounter them by the evidence of their tracks, or when my dog trees one of them in the dead of night. An exasperated, rasping, extraordinarily fierce growl from a low branch overhead announces that this is not another of the local forest animals—no silent coon, or hissing fisher, or muttering bear. In high summer and in the mating season, in February, the bobcats will sometimes exchange a few loud, declaratory screams.

Fishers are large relatives of the weasel. Like raccoons, they den in hollow trees, and leave their five-toed tracks when they lope through our small valley, which is notched into the south slope of the mountainside. In the winter they are especially on the prowl for porcupines, which they strip so cleanly of flesh and bone that only the flat skin remains, inside up, on the ground. Coons try to hole up in snowy weather, but porcupines remain more active. Fishers breed in March, right after the female's previous litter has been born. Porcupines breed in December, the male performing a clumsy, poignant, three-legged dance while clutching his testicles with one front paw. The colony of porcupines then winter quite sociably among boulders underneath spruce and birch. The mountain's band of deer, in the meantime, have crossed a hardwood ridge opposite the cliffs and gone down into a cedar woods alongside Big Valley Brook, a thousand feet lower, where they can chew the cedar bark and other favored foods, and where part of the snow, caught overhead in the thick screen of boughs, evaporates.

The coyotes who raise their pups across the notch from my house howl in the fall and winter months, but carefully keep mum during their denning season so as not to betray the location of their pups. In the spring, only the pups themselves are likely to break the silence of the den—and then only to yap wistfully for a moment in the middle of the night in answer to the yapping of our dog pup, when we have one.

June is the best time to see bears. Every other year, males from far and near come calling upon the sow who seems to make her headquarters in this notch. They are great romancing bachelors, and they roam the road in broad daylight, too impatient to wait till dusk. Her yearling cubs, whom she has already ceased to mother at the start of the courtship, must cast about incautiously for new quarters; you see them grazing in the field well past dawn and drinking at midday at the brook. The old bears welt some favorite birch-tree trunk, standing up and scratching competitively. Walking, one will notice the dead logs they have beaten apart in search of grubs; and if I have gotten just muzzy-headed enough after a hike of eight or a dozen miles and lean over a bashed log, I find myself experiencing some of the same hungry, busy, humdrum interest in what is there that the bear must have felt.

Behind the rock crest of the mountain is a pocket bog with pitcher plants. Also a spring which tumbles in upon itself in the form of a whirlpool, so that any leaf that you drop in promptly disappears. The deer summer in this high mixed woods of fir and spruce and birch and beech and maple, descending maybe half a mile at night to browse the patches of moosewood, hobblebush, fire cherry, mountain ash, shadblow, vetch, and wild apple saplings at the edge of the fields. A pair of red-tailed hawks nests each year somewhere along the whale's back, in trees that I have never located. There are broad-wingeds, too, and once in a while a goshawk. Barred owls bark at night, and ravens inhabit the cliffs, croaking eloquently at midmorning and in the afternoon—but not the marvelous peregrine falcons, or "ledge hawks," as the farmers used to call them. Forty years ago they would stunt during the spring courtship season with flirtatious giddy dives down from where the ravens flap.

Woodcock do a more modest but still spectacular swooping mating flight over a strip of alder thicket, where they later hunt earthworms. And below the alders is a beaver pond, which a pair of otters visits. Swimming playfully in sequence, they sometimes look to me like a sea monster. The patriarch among the beavers swims out toward them bravely and thwacks his tail on the water to warn his clan.

There are snowshoe rabbits, each intricately snug and custom-bound within the space of a handful of acres, bathing on a pleasant day in the same patch of dust that a ruffed grouse has used. And chipmunks—that courageous warning trill an individual, though hidden, gives, that may endanger it but save the race. There are congeries of song-birds, from indigo to scarlet-colored; three species of snakes in my woodpile; and trembling poplars, white-leaved in the wind, and all the manifestations of the moon.

1979

BICENTENNIAL
PALAVER

I have a hard time remembering whether the great man said, "Happy families are all alike; each unhappy family is unhappy in its own way," or the reverse. It was, of course, the first, but Tolstoy may have had more happy families to go by, whereas we see so many of the opposite kind that we find unhappiness commonplace. People put up with less rockiness in a marriage now, and the opportunity to dissolve a bad marriage in rather easy fashion tips plenty of marriages that are not really all that bad into court. They are *perceived* as bad. Dad, divorced, searching the movie page for someplace to roost with the kids next Sunday afternoon—it's hard to calculate any way that any good will come of this for anybody concerned. The New Life constructed at forty is a salvage operation, a desperate proposition, and when all of the romanticizing of desperate propositions is over with, there remains for most of us the distinct feeling that a good life on this earth should not need to be reconstructed at such a late date.

The aphorism which might apply is that everybody eventually gets not necessarily what he deserves but what he wants. This notion would strike most people as an absurdity if they were asked if it applied to them, and yet it's usually about as close as we are going to come to seeing justice done. So many individuals who lead lives fast and loose, when they confess in a rueful moment how they expect that everything will end for them, say they think they will wind up "all alone." Alone is how they've operated, at any rate; yet, still, they're likely to escape that fate simply because it isn't what they want.

Our difficulty, as well as our saving grace, is that most of us want contradictory things. We could begin, for example, by circling on a pollster's sheet one of the four traditional goals ambitious souls are said to hanker for: power, fame, "wimmin," or wealth. We might, too, accept the idea that power travels parallel to, instead of hand in hand with, fame; that wealth is a law unto itself; that women may be attracted to but are not held by wealth, power, or fame. And so, recognizing one primary goal, we could plan to renounce the other three where they seemed to conflict—except that we'd weaken, naturally, just as the politician does who wants his sexual liaisons and flirts wretchedly with scandal, or wants more money and fudges up his income taxes; like the rich man collecting art at the expense of his business interests, in order to perpetuate his name; or the artist growing sick of being poor even as he begins to win some straightforward fame.

There is a saying, though, that "you can't be too rich or too thin." There are people who are congenitally cheerful, who can turn their hand to almost anything, who "know how to live," people who manage quite happily to do contradictory things. In school they realized right away that in order to be popular you have to attract attention, but if you attract too much attention you will be unpopular. They have excellent marriages that afford them a great deal of happiness, yet enjoy an occasional amorous affair. They know that if a man lies dying as fierce as a hawk, angry at his illness, people will remember him affectionately, but if he dies lovingly and uncomplainingly, they will remember him fondly also. Once at a party I met an astronaut, famous for his flights through space, who had just bicycled for a hundred and forty miles through the hills of Vermont —a high executive at Space Headquarters, though he was coiffed and costumed like the weaver dropouts who were there. All that was different about him was his determined eye.

To live smoothly is to hold to a course of decency but not idealism, and such people are in their element in the midst of the paradoxes that make for good living. They abound in public life and the upper echelons of the professions, and, apart from their tailoring, cannot be told from their Soviet counterparts in the group photographs that are taken to commemorate an exchange tour or a state visit, because the same sort of person, fitting himself to the circumstances, will hold the same position in a dictatorship as in a democracy.

But as it happens, what we need at the moment is for these many leaders (or at least a few of them) to enunciate plainly and publicly the paradoxes that the country lives with, speaking gaily and even confidently, the way men of affairs do when they speak among themselves of the sea of paradoxes through which they swim in their own lives and in making decisions. Instead of the sort of resilient candor one would get from the best of them in conversation, they divide up when talking for public consumption and tell us either that everything important is the same as it always was for America, or, on the contrary, that nothing will ever again be the same.

Two freedoms were emphasized at the time of our founding: freedom of speech and the freedom to get rich. This set up a permanent torsion in our foreign policy—our wish to get rich at the expense of freedom in less industrialized countries—and, here at home, a comic incompatibility between the contingent of souls who have done rather well for themselves and those who haven't and who exercise their right to complain. America, as we conceived it, was not for *being* rich so much as for *getting* rich. Unlike Old World wealth, there was supposed to be an onward thrust to it, which has become harder to maintain as the nation has aged. A supremely mercantile country, we know how to abide by a written compact—which gives the Constitution its remarkable force—and yet here, as elsewhere, democracy travesties itself even in purest form, as any New Englander who goes to town meetings knows. A revolutionary country no longer in need of a revolution, we have forgotten our beginnings, and, besides, have other pungent legends —cowpokes, mountainmen, rivermen—we don't know what to make of now. We shoot at our public figures, but somehow this practice is less disturbing than our habit of voting landslide victories to Presidents who thereupon must be forced out of office. Our famous ethnic condiments have turned rather lumpy in the cooking pot, confusing the traditionalists among us; and when we stop advocating busing to eliminate racial segregation in the public schools, our minds are sufficiently single-track that we're likely to stop being in favor of integration itself.

The country is big enough that within a single state New York City is partly countervailed by Homer and

Rome, New York—a bulk and variety that over the years has helped to absorb some of the shocks. The North has been a corrective to the South and the East to the West, yet we have been able to expand west and south. Loathing our penchant for violence but loyal to our violent myths, we nurse our bruises from the decade just past and, as these start to heal and itch, want to repudiate the whole reformist endeavor. We hardly need to mock the remaining mugwumps of the Left, they so often parody themselves, converting to some new panacea or trotting off to the jailhouse for shoplifting or a drug bust. As a nation we need to idle and recharge, but there seems to be no time to do this. Part of a writer's job is to swim upstream, much in the way that a trader does who buys when prices are low and sells when they are high again and so keeps the world going around. Writers unearth ideas that have been laid aside, reaffirm the unfashionable, on this same principle that we swim in a sea of paradoxes among which we snatch up first one, then another, being unable to chew gum and scratch ourselves at the same time. But with no present consensus about what is generally held to be true, writers have no back wall to toe off from.

So, we wanted a rest, and we aren't going to get a rest, and what we need now is a politician who can say just exactly that with a laugh. He ought to say that every which way that we're pulled may wind up being useful if we remember the spirit of generosity and pragmatism in which we originally started. He should be not many things to different people but many things within himself. Pragmatism and generosity, too, are contradictory qualities, and yet they're the hope of the world.

1976

HEADING OUT
FROM HOME

To live is to see, and traveling sometimes speeds up the process. In Khartoum this winter I ran into an old acquaintance unexpectedly in the hotel lobby. He had been a year behind me in college, and now in his mid-forties, he was to set off at five o'clock the next morning to visit the Eritrean guerrillas in northern Ethiopia, just as I was about to entrain in the opposite direction to the Darfur desert to see the camel-riding Kababish nomads near the Libyan border—two rather arduous writing assignments for different publishing organizations, which we both turned out to have sought, indeed. He had a bullfrog in his throat and had only just recuperated from a serious operation, so that although I can't vouch for how I looked, he was wan and puckery. I had been into Eritrea very briefly myself—the guerrillas were begging for publicity—but the last American reporter who had undertaken the full trek had lost seventeen pounds during the experience, according to the United States Information Service man based in Khartoum. That had been three years ago, and the last British newspaperman, much more recently, had wound up being seized as a hostage himself. Though we knew that such a fate probably wouldn't befall my friend, our grins over our drinks were appropriately ambivalent and middle-aged.

This is not the place to recount his adventures or mine, but by good fortune we ran into each other again a month later as we were both about to catch a plane out of Khartoum. He looked exactly the same—neither well nor unwell —and although he was wearing a cheerful T-shirt inscribed with the word for journalist in Arabic, he had lost his voice all over again as a result of being caught in a rainstorm on his last night in Eritrea. I, too, had discovered—just as I had earlier, down in the high rain forest on the Sudanese border with Uganda—the difference that fifteen or twenty years' aging makes in exhausting journeys of the kind. We were both heartily sick of eating sorghum mush with our fingers out of a common bowl, of sleeping on the ground and hearing revolutionary theory from fighters young enough to be our sons, listening to them boast of battles not yet fought, and visualizing their disillusionment in another few years. Still, despite our renewed irony, our grins were real enough, because that had been the point of it—to bring minds that were already near fifty to Africa.

What I am getting at, however, is that we, or the likes of us, seemed to be the only foreign observers hanging around. A young reporter for *The New York Times* had shown up for a couple of days, but had had to return to Cairo. The year before, in East Africa, I had encountered only one young American journalist, Tony Avirgan, *Time* magazine's stringer in Dar-es-Salaam. Where were the writers turning thirty or so who ought to be pouring into this pyro-technic continent? You understand, this is no Hemingway-esque complaint. Hemingway is as dead as Britannia in Africa, and my friend and I, in any case, are ten years younger than that last generation of writers—Norman Mailer, Peter Matthiessen, and so on—whose vision is occa-sionally distorted by a romancifying like Hemingway's. It was the idea that to live is to see that had brought us to Africa, not some punctilious concern about manly behavior.

Nevertheless—that said—why on earth should our gaunt, quite endearing, Afro-headed Eritrean revolutionaries need to beg through the hotels of Khartoum for a Western wit-ness to go with them into their mountain stronghold? If young writers actually have stopped heading out from home, it is a sad and silly development, a fallout both from the catastrophe of Vietnam and from the sex war now sput-tering in America, where people are confused about their life "roles." Many older intellectuals have a peevish reaction to any mention of the Third World because of various United Nations votes and speeches—which is a know-noth-ing response to know-nothingism, as if a foreign minister's United Nations rhetoric had the faintest connection with the true life of his country. But what matters more than the mind-set of older intellectuals is that so many young writers seem to be staying home. For them it is not a question of choice or of ideology. Instead, it is a form of limpness, an in-turning that is most unfortunate both for them and for us.

I have specific memories from the borders of Uganda, Ethiopia, and Libya, where I was in the midst of stark and sharply illustrative, extended little African dramas, and where a younger observer could have picked up after my stamina ran out and I had to leave off. Tony Avirgan last year not only was *Time*'s stringer in Dar-es-Salaam, but telexed almost daily reports to the Associated Press and United Press International (transmitting a slightly different wording for each story to each wire service, giving precedence one day to one, the next day to the other). He also wrote for a London newspaper, and did frequent broadcasts for the British Broadcasting Company. As talented and dedicated a journalist as Avirgan is, that so much work was thrust upon him would seem to indicate that there is a shortage of Western witnesses in Africa right now.

1977

CAIRO
OBSERVED

The traffic going around Liberation Square in the center of Cairo used to be described as the circles of hell; and it's not that it's no longer scary but that they've built a great circular walkway for pedestrians up above, where everybody afoot strides freely along. As in any metropolis when the traffic is somehow surmounted for the moment, it's an exuberant sensation being up there—seven-league boots and so on. To climb, anyway, is a triumph of Islam. The muezzin mounts high in his minaret to call the faithful to prayer, while the Christian sexton stands down below his church steeple, tugging a rope to ring the church bell. Of old Egypt, too: the first minaret is said to have been built in Cairo, and it was Cheops who, in the twenty-seventh century B.C., conceived of his pyramid, not as a huge deadweight gravestone, but (changing in mid-plan) as a monument far up into which his architects climbed to construct a lofty burial chamber above the ground.

Cars seem to have just been invented here, mostly the so-called Nasser cars, a modified Fiat manufactured in Egypt. A tattoo of horns, silvery or peevish, "the music of Cairo," fills the air around the clock, like ten thousand weddings, ten thousand bridegrooms. Really the cars as well as the drivers are talking, and underneath all the emotional clamor are the other spirits of Africa's largest city, fifth largest capital in the world: the roosters and goats people keep on their roofs; the painted tea carts; the roast-yam, roast-corn, sugarcane vendors; the jingling horse wagons heaped up with olives, cabbages, oranges, leeks, barrels of fuel oil, building stone—a glazier's wagon thrusting through a medieval dirt alley; mile upon mile of mud-brick houses baked from the hot silt of the Nile. A million babies a year are born in Egypt; and Cairo, like Mexico City or Jakarta or comparable cities, is jammed with youngsters. A few street dogs to stagger about, trying to live on the juices the garbage pickers can't salvage, but in three weeks of walking I saw not much hunger. The government subsidizes by three-fourths the price of wheat, so that a filling flat breakfast loaf costs only the equivalent of about a penny, a bowl of beans another penny, and a little serving of tomatoes and onions to go with them another penny or two.

I was there during Kourban Bairam, which is the annual occasion for pilgrimages and the sacred holiday when Muslims recapitulate the commitment to God that Abraham, "the first Muslim," made by sacrificing a sheep, after first having offered his son. Paddle-tailed sheep were tied up all over town; and citified men in blue suits and sun-whipped

Bedouin in brown galabiehs were carrying these home on their shoulders for the ceremony, as we lug a Christmas tree. Indeed, any time meat is on sale in Cairo there is a certain excitement. Because of the shortage of land for livestock it's sold only two days a week.

Ramadan, a fast-feast, though a lesser religious event, has a seesaw or frenzied edge, people sitting with a tumbler of orange juice, waiting for the cannon to boom over Cairo marking sunset, when they can quench their thirst. The fasting begins at dawn when one can distinguish a black from a white thread; and it's a month for parties, making the night day. The meals served then are the best of the year, a fast being a marvelous condiment. A good many offices close early (official Cairo goes home at 2:00 P.M. anyhow), so that everybody can catch up on his or her sleep and, as much as possible, escape from the irritable, hungry hours. The neighborhood fire-eater promenades down the street, along with a character balancing three chairs on his nose.

Kourban Bairam broadcasts a steadier din: the kids in new clothes with cherry bombs and toy drums who ride the street swing that a dusty, fat donkey hauls around, stopping at each market square where there is a piaster to be made, eating carrot tops in the interlude. There's a merry-go-round that a stick-boned man revolves by leaning his shoulder into a leather sling while beating a pair of cymbals also. His old father, with an eye disease that means he can't blink, keeps the kids in line with a little stick. The donkey is beaten on the same muscles it pulls with, but is thriving, apparently. One proud man leads the big dog-tailed sheep he has bought to the bank of the Nile to wash it, washing his knife and his butchering boots too. In the poorer quarters the meat sold is all legs and heads, of assorted lengths

—both goat and cow. The butcher stews them in a black tub until he can scrape the hair off, then simmers them till a customer comes. Dealing with the heads, he cuts an animal's gums loose from its skull, and, putting his mouth to the goat's or cow's mouth, blows very hard, till the cheeks balloon free of the bones; then lets it quietly float and cook.

I sat with one such man for a couple of hours, next to a half-dozen vegetable stalls, a live-goat market, a merry-go-round, a peddler's cart of spaghetti and rice, and another of sweetmeats, yogurt, and cakes. We were in an open square in Bulaq, a district of Cairo that likes to claim it's so tough it has been the flashpoint of revolution in Egypt. The elders leave barbells outside on stools so the local young hardies can perform a few hefts each time they walk by. Two of the butcher's daughters were with us, just as girls will hang about their father's store anywhere, with some friends of theirs, around fourteen years old. We sat on crates, the sun was hot, and rancid garbage was heaped up nearby, and yet it seemed both natural and civilized to be sitting there, as though we were indoors. Talking to him, watching him work—a pleasant, bustly, middle-class sort of man—I kept thinking that, transposed to my own country, instead of selling cow shins and cheeks from a boiling cauldron set in a slum square, he might be managing a power substation for Con Edison or a small branch bank. On the other hand, the poverty wasn't so bad that anybody was hanging around to beg a sip of the bloody broth, which, when he'd finished, he emptied onto the ground.

A woman was beating her rugs overhead, and when a good-looking girl walked by, the barbell crowd whispered, "Isis!"—the fertile goddess. (A "lioness," by contrast, is a prostitute in Arabic slang.) The cartmen hissed too, more sharply, to clear a path for their donkeys. And all over

town, reverberating by loudspeaker, the imams were beam-
ing prayers from the mud-colored mosques to worshipers
crouched in the street—mosques fort-walled among the low
buildings. In counterpoint, whole fleets of cars wheeled
about Cairo blaring a code of toots that identified them as
rooting for one or the other of the soccer teams playing in
the stadium that afternoon.

Cairo is a walker's city, the two essential conditions for
walking being well satisfied: that you can drink the water,
and that no one in any neighborhood, although you may
have what amounts to a year's worth of wages in your
pocket, is going to knock you over the head. Tourists can't
usually be quite so carefree about food, but "What doesn't
kill you will fatten you," the saying goes. The wheat beer is
mild, the Nile has zigzag-masted feluccas on it, and white
ibises and black kites sail in the sky. The trees are palms,
mangoes, tamarisks, and pines—alive in the evening with
screaming birds.

Boxy yellow-and-red antiquated trolley cars roll you
about for a fare of a couple of cents, ending up eventually
in the desert sand, unless you drop off in the meantime and
stroll. Milk is delivered by bicycle, and bread by a boy ped-
aling through traffic balancing three loaded trays on his
free hand. Carrot juice and cane syrup are squeezed to
order and sold on the street, along with steel wool, sheep's
wool, eels, eating-oranges, and bream. A pinkish water
buffalo calf is going to market—veal here is buffalo veal.
There's a set of scales in the street; for half a piaster you
weigh yourself. A taxicab passes by with a glass chandelier
mounted on the roof and a dead mongoose lying on the
back shelf. The hearses have eight wooden angels painted
silver poised up on top.

It's a magnificent city as seen from the minaret of the Ibn

Tulun Mosque. Below, a grown buffalo has got loose in the street, and meets an oblivious camel loaded with cauliflower. (The Nubians brought elephants down the Nile even before the Arabs brought camels.) The few high buildings are isolated from each other and airy and personable, and the earthen colors of the rest of the structures lend an aura of age or dignity to the nondescript sections of town. Most sections are nondescript, in the sense that dust blows and the houses are constantly being rebuilt or in need of repair. The people swarm—always the children, Cairo's triumph and pain. Pushing toward a population of eight million, many of them rubes from the delta, others refugees from the blitzed Suez region, this is a city where people don't yet know where they are or whether their lives will be long or short. The poor have been inundated by more poor, and so the majesty of the place simply consists of the heat and piled-up colors of so much concentrated life, and, all around, the loud, ringing ages of Egypt. Strange, narrow, tall, yellow-washed, arabesque tenements, with pigeons whirling above the dovecotes, back up against the battlemented brown towers of a half-ruined mosque looming higher still. There is a mosque for every four buses in Cairo; and thirteen hundred years of hovels have been piled atop former hovels.

In the morning, you wake to the jingle of harnesses, a splat of rain, and, briefly, a rainbow over the river. Turn a block or two almost anywhere and it's the fifteenth century—a close alleyway with leaning balconies, where the women let down a basket to shop. A peddler dashes alongside his mare with a hand on her hip, a cartload of dried fish rattling behind, a mound of horse-drawn bananas coming his way, and another wagon loaded with chickens in crates, with turkeys tied individually by the feet on top—a boy and a hare-footed dog dodging past. A restaurateur has set up a bench at one side of the street and is serving buffalo liver with bran. Even camel meat is eaten—though it's full of water—by the hungry, and a roast-yam man has collected a handful of sticks from the Nile for his baby-sized stove. Egyptians like to nibble when they can afford to. Another entrepreneur is offering chickpeas in paper cones, and lupine, pumpkin, watermelon, and sunflower seeds nicely toasted.

There is a specificity to life in Islam that Christianity used to have too, in different form. The month begins not mathematically but when two "reliable observers," now in Arabia but previously in every area, can testify that they have seen the sliver of the new moon. And when the believer with a prayer callus on his forehead prostrates himself toward Mecca five times a day, he actually faces in that direction, although most of the rest of us would not be able to tell east from north nowadays.

Calcutta is the bugaboo my expatriate friends mentioned repeatedly—affectionate Arabists and Egyptologists, twenty-year veterans of Cairo's emergencies, who want the best for the country and hope to see it tip into equilibrium. The problem is that in the next quarter-century the population of Egypt will grow to something like seventy (from thirty-seven) million, with only an original skinny strip of six million tillable acres along the Nile—desert everywhere else. Thanks to the dam at Aswan, a million and a half more acres have been refurbished from the old floodplain by a laborious procedure of drainage or irrigation and rice planting to remove the salts. Perhaps another two million can be reclaimed. Unfortunately, most of this new land is marginal and eats up fertilizer, whereas some of the historic breadbasket of Egypt is being converted to urban sprawl—a projected loss of twenty to sixty thousand acres a year, I was told.

Nile wheat had been Egypt's bounty until the British administrators switched much of her wheat land to cotton during the nineteenth century to support England's textile mills, a priority she has retained because she now needs the foreign exchange. Though the limited strip of black land irrigated by the river is extraordinarily productive—an average of thirty-five hundred pounds of food grains per acre sown—the nation's industry must be multiplied tenfold to buy enough food to feed all of the people who will live here in twenty-five years. Egypt's foreign policy is partly predicated upon providing the city poor with hundreds of millions of dollars in "soft"-loaned American grain; and the cotton, flax, fresh fruit, flowers, onions, and garlic she exports are also buying time. The Suez Canal is the chief hard-money earner, apart from cotton; oil next (and will supplant them); then tourism, which can't help but expand if peace prevails. Dredging the canal for bigger tankers may raise revenues by six hundred million dollars a year, and Egypt's own oil production should reach a million dollars a day by 1980.

Anwar Sadat is described as a petit bourgeois by the radical Arabs, an appellation that sometimes seems fair when one trudges through Cairo's traffic congestion—the private cars belonging to people who buried their money in the Nasser years, when the government would have seized it, and have now dug it up. One of the amazing, even "jolly," sights to a tourist in the city for the first time is the incredible scrimmage at every bus stop, morning and afternoon—the struggle to get on. During the worst couple of hours only young men in their prime make it at all, and then only by sprinting alongside the bus for a block before it reaches the stop and vaulting against the jam of people already stuffed in the open door. They ride crabbed on the back bumper or half in, half out of the windows; and the women, the older people, sit on the curbstone into the evening hours. Their expressions, as one sees them condemned to sit there while their children and chores await them at home, give a sad cast to Cairo.

Laborers, shop clerks earn perhaps twenty dollars a month; Ph.D.'s, cabdrivers, thirty dollars; engineers, full professors, seventy-five dollars. The government bureaucrats whom one meets feel it necessary to save into their thirties before they have accumulated enough money to get married. The reason—and part of the impetus that produced Sadat's Open Door policy toward the West—is that there are too few jobs for the numbers of people. Three helpers wait on you in a store, where one would be plenty; three or four government workers—guaranteed jobs if they are university graduates—occupy empty desks in every cubicle in the Mogamma, the huge central office building downtown.

It's said that Sadat and Nasser, because of their rashness, each "divided" and "united" the Arabs. Nasser inspired the radicals, who in Lebanon still act in his name, but Sadat brought around the then leery oil monarchs and sheikhs to an alliance with Egypt, which made possible not only his own quasi-victory in the October War but gave the royalists their worldwide leverage through OPEC in the years afterwards. For Egypt it was essential that the 1973 war be fought and won, because the Israelis, sitting on the banks of the Suez Canal after a victory six years before that had been just as crucial for them, had formed the peculiar opinion that it was in their best interest to see Cairo gradually turn into Calcutta and starve.

Nasser had helped depose King Farouk in 1952, and decisively evicted the British, as the revolt of 1919 and the negotiations of 1936 had not been able to do. He redistributed landholdings of more than two hundred acres into small plots, leveled the worst of the other social inequities, and squeezed out the miscellany of Greek, Italian, and Lebanese businessmen who had dominated the economy before. The new economy he organized on an austere basis leading toward self-sustainment—Egyptian ready-made suits, canned goods, refrigerators—away from dependence upon European imports. He built up the army, giving the nation a sense of destiny and pride, de-emphasizing at the same time the muzzier nationalism that had staked for Egypt simply the claim of being "oldest in the world." Though he is criticized now for wasting both blood and treasure in a war in Yemen ("In Yemen!" the Egyptians, who are terrible snobs, will exclaim) and tipping his country into the Six-Day War with Israel but not getting his air force off the ground, he was a pan-Arab figure who galvanized the imagination of people clear from Morocco to the Persian Gulf —the first such for many years.

Meanwhile, the Americans, who had befriended him by their neutrality during the Suez War in 1956, unaccountably conceived the idea that they could better maintain a position of influence in the Middle East from out at the perimeter, in wildest Baghdad, and accordingly had dumped the Aswan Dam project (a painful slice of history that the Russians seem bent on repeating from their present unsteady foothold in Damascus and Baghdad). Came the Russians. Came Sadat. Sadat saw that although only the

71

Nasser connection with the Soviets had enabled Egypt to seize the east bank of the Suez from Israel in 1973—the Soviets threatening to parachute troops to his aid when the Israelis reversed his initiative—the West could do more for him now. Only the United States could provide the wheat he needed; and the Western powers, high-pressure, booster infusions of technology. This complicated changeover he accomplished with much finesse, with Henry Kissinger's assistance, patiently monitoring in the meantime the slide in Nasser's reputation. He still is dogged by a Nasserite-socialist element in the bureaucracy that is slow to cooperate with Western businessmen, but he made no impolitic moves, such as purging the Mogamma offices of Nasser's picture. Instead, he saw installed as head of the mass-circulation newspaper *Al Akhbar* a right-wing editor who had been imprisoned and tortured by Nasser's police. Though Sadat may be remembered as a national, not pan-Arab, leader vis-à-vis Nasser, his best, or most interesting, hours so far* have occurred in those two early years when he was being mocked as a softie, a waffler, by the radical Arabs and gibed at by Golda Meir and some of his countrymen, when he seemed to have nothing in mind at all, but was actually negotiating simultaneously with Syria's President Assad, with the Kremlin, and Saudi Arabia's king.

The soldiers of Egypt's First Army, who still believe it was American pilots, not Israelis, who bombed them in the closing days of the October War, as the Americans' resupply effort surpassed the Russians', will tell you that "God stood by." The tragic fascination of the conflict has been not only that each side regarded it as Biblical, a *jihad* fought across old battlefields, but that these two peoples—

*Before his trip to Jerusalem.

unlike, for example, the Greek and Turkish Cypriots—are not merely murderous in their view of each another. A visit to partitioned Cyprus is a tedious experience, because, first of all, one knows the holocausts that the Turks have inflicted upon minorities in the past, and yet remembers that the Cypriot Greeks, too, when the world was not looking, have seemed to set themselves the task of snuffing out the life of every Turk. The Israelis have proven to be notably gentle conquerors, however. And the Arabs—although they have everywhere made a habit of reducing Jewish or Christian communities to second-class status within the Muslim state, like Egypt's Copts—do not seek final solutions. To put the matter more starkly, it can be said that if the Jews who went to Europe during the Diaspora had remained in the Arab countries, there would be six million more human beings alive.

Nobody can visit Israel without becoming pro-Israeli. No one with a neutral eye can look at that oddly serene and resilient nation and not wish for it to survive. But the extraordinary empathy I felt in Egypt was significant also —as the Israelis I met in Jerusalem on the next leg of my trip who had served with the British in Cairo during World War II confirmed. The point about Cairo is the *thronging*, the feeling of all humanity precariously rushing by. Copts with marvelously forceful, disdainful, fastidious noses that center the face as the noses of the pharaohs in funerary sculpture do; then the fellow who has flattened his nose by balancing chairs on it; and a desert rat with a slim wary face all eyes and ears under his checkered kaffiyeh. The crowds pour down the street shouting, or reverse directions, as the traffic does, and the traffic is such a happy great beast much of the time that one hardly resents it. Late at night the only beggars are a few women making a bed of the sidewalk, each with her children around her. She covers all of herself except one cupped hand and all but the children's sleeping faces with a black cloth, as if she had cast herself not at your feet but on the mercy of God.

Many Americans, who perhaps regard Jews as wogs, consider the Arabs even more woggish than Jews, and the result has been a danger that America's tilt toward Israel will become an excuse to shut our ears to the calls for help of dozens of poor nations, if they differ with us politically on the Middle East, and we are looking for a pretext to let them go hungry anyway. Some of the Israelis, too, because of their swift victories, had come to regard the Arabs as wogs. It may be that for Israel's well-being she needed to lose.

The Egyptians won back their self-esteem. Newsmen, businessmen, tourists flocked in. (The Bedouin at the Giza pyramids had started to kill off their camels for want of sightseers to ride them.) Columnists like Joseph Kraft, who before the war had written about the menace of "Arabists" in the State Department who might have us take into account the Arab viewpoint, suddenly started filing columns from Beirut. Now the Egyptians could give expression to their irritation with the Palestinians, Iraqis, and other shrill voices removed from the battlefield whose wars they were sick of fighting "to the last Egyptian," as they said. I heard this impatience so often, I became convinced of the truth of what the officials told me: that Egypt accepts the existence of Israel, that "pushing the Israelis into the sea" is a notion discredited, that peace is possible between the two countries once the Israelis return the Sinai, but that since the Israelis cannot feel safe about doing so until they conclude what will remain an uneasy peace with the Palestinians by agreeing to a Palestinian state on the Jordan's West

Bank, it will all take some time. When they are asked if an economic pact with Israel wouldn't help, the Egyptians say the bitterness is too sharp for that now, that Israel's technology is "derivative," besides, and why not go to the source.

A planner in the Ministry of Industry drew three boxes linked by a triangle to show me where his nation's hopes were pinned. One was labeled "Money (Oil States). " Another, "Technology," meant the West. "People," the third, was Egypt itself. Egypt, five times as populous as Syria or Saudi Arabia, could furnish an enormous market for goods and services if only its people can somehow be jacked into consumer status, and as he spoke about that possibility, the pinch of the dilemma of feeding everybody went out of my planner friend's face. Egyptians are good metallurgists and electricians, and already export TV sets and air conditioners. They say with enough foreign help they could make their country the manufacturing center of the Arab world. The trouble is that Western businessmen find Cairo a madhouse personally and a bureaucratic morass. To reach Alexandria by telephone may take five hours, let alone trying to get through to London or New York. Even local phone service is apt to blank out by ten in the morning. The Saudis, for their part, are assisting Egypt to pay off its arms debt to Russia, but, naturally,would rather bring workmen to Jidda and pay them twenty-five dollars a day to build factories there than a dollar a day in Cairo to help set up the sort of industrial facilities within Egypt that might dwarf the Saudis' efforts at home.

In the face of my friend is a generic softness, a remarkable look, as was the case with the other officials I met—you can see it in pictures of Anwar Sadat in conference with Kissinger—although because of the Cairene penchant for wearing dark glasses, you must wait for the glasses to come off. Egyptians are a hierarchical people who take to a central authority, having had more than three thousand years of that. They have known so many conquerors—Napoleon, Caesar, Alexander, not to mention Muslims like Amr, from Arabia, and Saladin, a Kurd—that they still seem to look for a man on horseback to show them the way, as Kissinger has, perhaps.

"Well-cum!" Abousef the cabby exclaims. "Well-cum to Egypt!" as if there had been a radio campaign to teach him the words—but with enthusiasm. Even if he is hustling you, he will interrupt the hustle to announce "Well-cum to Egypt," as if to tell you, This hustle I am attempting to put over on you is one of the humiliations of poverty.

"They'll kill you there!" he says, glancing into the rear-view mirror on the ride from the airport to see whether he is persuading you to cancel your reservations and come instead to the hotel where he gets a cut. Each traffic light is personally managed by a policeman, but somebody is always changing a tire at an intersection, and when the traffic stalls, Abousef backs up and turns right around against the one-way stream to get clear of it. Some of the taxis are flatbed wagons, twenty women shawled in black going to market. They are veilless, but bite their head shawls when a foreigner looks at them so as to feel the reassurance of a veil across the mouth again. Others side-sit a donkey, balancing a basket of figs on the head.

The girls paint their eyelids green or white. The men go barefoot or wear plastic sandals or shoes, depending upon their station in life. Jammed into a row of holes-in-the-wall are welding and soldering establishments, tinkers' stalls, chairsmiths' stalls, a barbershop partly set up in the street.

A fellow in a tarboosh is selling two catfish still kicking in a pail. A donkey is heaped with pomegranates, eggplant, zucchini. There are wagons of sponges, brooms, bolts of cloth, a wagon of tame ducks and rabbits in crates, of skinned sheep heads, each with a lettuce leaf stuffed into its mouth. The sprawling gray shantytowns overlap even into the old mosques and cemeteries.

I walked till my legs swelled up and the sand split the seams of my shoes, not learning much Arabic but learning its angry sound—like Hebrew gone angry—though in Egypt it really isn't angry at all. *"Ma'alaysh"* ("Never mind") is the national expression. The Crusaders got to the Nile but didn't reach Cairo. It wasn't traded back and forth, as Jerusalem and Damascus were, and was never taken by Tamerlane or Hulagu Khan, who over on the Euphrates (now Iraq) constructed whole pyres of human skulls. Except for Napoleon and the British, after the original Muslim conquest of 641 its conquerors—Fatimid, Mameluke, Turk—have been coreligionists.

Historically, Syria has been something of a sister country to Egypt, quarreling with her but otherwise leaning on her to countervail the powerful armies of the Tigris and Euphrates valleys, which longed to gobble Syria up. Egypt's special coherence was a gift of the Nile. Its people were settled farmers, taxed for centuries at a rate arrived at by calculating the level of the river, who could be easily ruled from a single capital. First it was Memphis, then Thebes, then Alexandria. Syria, by contrast, consisted of a string of rival city-states—Aleppo, Damascus, Jerusalem, Jaffa—and still is bedeviled by fragmentation, although a certain democratic spirit results. The boss on a construction project in Syria will work right alongside his men, whereas in Egypt there is much bowing and salaaming to the "doctor" in a ministry office, the "director" of a business. A gentleman farmer in Egypt is likely to call himself an "agricultural engineer."

Egypt is 90 percent Sunni Muslim and 10 percent Christian, thereby escaping the divisive Sunni-Shi'ite split that plagues Iraq in particular and Lebanon and Syria also. Iraq, for all the fertility of its great river valleys, has always had feral mountain tribes like the Kurds to contend with, and was sandwiched between the Ottoman and Persian empires—unkindly foes who battled across it for four hundred years—as if being on one of the Mongols' main invasion routes wasn't trouble enough. Iraq, as a consequence, is frenetic still. Lebanon has constituted a juggler's joke of Sunnis, Shi'ites, Druzes, Kurds, Alaouites, Armenians, Circassians, Maronite Christians, Palestinian exiles, and half a dozen other potentially inimical sects. Jordan is another deaccessioned wedge of colonial geography; and Algeria and Morocco are an amalgam of feud-prone tribal groups, Berber versus Arab. Tunisia hasn't yet resolved the question of whether it is unqualifiedly North African or partly French. Libya lies partially in Tunisia's sphere of influence, partially in Egypt's, and considerably under the spell of the Sahara itself.

Because of this fractionation, and ever since the Mongols' destruction of Baghdad in the thirteenth century, Cairo has been the hub of Islamic learning, the seat of Al-Azhar and now Cairo universities. Altogether, four hundred thousand students from various countries are enrolled in colleges in Egypt, and educated Egyptians, when their patience with regional squabbles wears thin, are not above describing the Saudis as "primitives," the Libyans as "monsters" and "beasts," the Iraqis as "savages," "sadists." In fact, it's said the principal reason why Nasser's experiment at uniting the Egyptian and Syrian nations in 1958 didn't succeed was that thousands of know-it-all Egyptian civil servants suddenly turned up in Damascus, fussy and correct, to set everyone straight. Egyptians are a source of administrative talent through much of the Middle East, yet, as an Iraqi surgeon remarked to me, the Iraqis can understand the Cairenes' Arabic perfectly well but the Cairenes appear to have trouble understanding Iraqis.

Iraq, Syria, and the Sudan have no looming famine problem on the horizon, however, as Egypt does. In rural Egypt the peasants have learned to eat corn bread in lieu of wheat, and make do with overcooked tea for a narcotic when they are hungry, or bread beer, date wine, fermented potato skins. Water buffalo is the chief milk-meat animal, as well as turning the water wheels everywhere, but the fellahin are the despair of the Agriculture Ministry because for reasons of superstition they will not eat buffalo meat (*gamoose*) that was butchered at more than forty days old. And a herdsman's best sheep are likely to be dedicated to God at the feast of Kourban Bairam, not saved as breeding stock. Beef is not subject to such derailments of the planning process, and the ministry hopes to develop areas of the western desert as a Texas-type cattle range if it can.

The authorities are bringing in Frisian dairy cows too, and want to manufacture their own fertilizer and pesticides from native petroleum and phosphates, with Japanese help. The construction industry must be revolutionized so that Egypt's bricks are not baked in primitive kilns from the richest topsoil laid down by the Nile, but out of waste sand in higher-heat kilns. New rolling stock is needed for the railroad. A paper industry should be created to make use of an abundance of sugarcane husks, and a plastics industry for the Abu Rudeis oil. Battery, ketchup, and tire factories are needed, and more cement plants and cotton mills. The steel and aluminum complexes that the Russians built must be retooled; Australian bauxite is being shipped in. An Italian company is assisting with a 450-kilometer Suez–Mediterranean pipeline, and Westinghouse with a new power plant for Cairo itself. Soon the electricity generated by the Aswan Dam will be fully spoken for, so that the government's current pie in the sky has to do with a geological phenomenon called the Qattara Depression. This Switzerland-sized Death Valley sinks more than four hundred feet below sea level. In theory, a canal could bring seawater tumbling through a gigantic generator at a pace that just equaled the evaporation, and power all Egypt.

In the fields by the Nile, cotton, corn, rice, and melons are harvested during the summer, and, in winter, flax, barley, wheat, citrus fruits, and bananas, plus two crucial legumes—clover and broad beans—that not only replenish the soil with nitrogen but are the staff of life for livestock and man. But maybe 80 percent of the peasants still suffer from bilharzia, the weakening disease borne by snails in slow-moving irrigation water. Just as many can't read or write, although the proportion is smaller among the young. In the decade from 1960 to 1970 the yearly birth rate declined from forty-two to thirty-five infants per thousand Egyptians, but in a peasant society more children have always meant more hands for the harvest, and so to completely reverse this ancient concept of prosperity is going to take time. Islam proper must adjust to the idea that there are other things for women to do besides having children.

Such rocky obstacles, such urgent quandaries, when the present xenophobia within the United States about the "developing countries" has subsided, will draw many Americans to Africa. It used to be that we asked about an expatriate, What's the matter with him that he couldn't measure up to the mark back home? But rather soon, just as so many English are doing, we ourselves are going to be leaving in droves, looking for challenges that seem real, where life isn't programmed.

I'd come from London and Rome, where the foreign communities are feeling dispirited, inclined to clear out. The Romans have "bought back their city"; it no longer belongs to its visitors, as it used to. Nor is anybody's money much good. Metal coins fly across the Swiss border by the ton to make watch casings, and you're handed a lemon, a bun, instead, in the store, for change. Londoners, too, have lost faith in themselves, so that the expatriate Americans who thought they had cleverly positioned themselves at midstream in the world find themselves floating off in an oxbow. They complain of British politeness and self-mockery, the stopped clock on every street corner. But the Americans in Egypt, from the sampling I met, felt vindicated and are remarkably united in rooting for the country. Whatever they came for originally—whether winter sunshine or pederasty—might have been obtained more conveniently in Rome; yet they pressed on to Cairo and have a lighter step here. Their sympathies have taken root.

Arabists are an intriguing lot. Some no doubt are anti-Jewish. Hearing an elderly fellow with a Germanic accent say that "for various reasons" he hasn't visited Jerusalem since it was captured by the Israelis, one wonders what those reasons *are*. Others, in contrast, are Jews who may have begun their studies years ago with the hope of bridging two cultures, but who, disheartened now, have turned their scholarship quite frankly to propaganda and intelligence work. The Arabists in Cairo whom I took a liking to, however, had in common an element of Walter Mitty in them. They love the harsh-sounding, vowelly syllables of the language, and patiently endure "eight months of summer" and the bouts of "intestinal flu," as they like to call the intestinal disorders that go with the privilege of hearing those vowels on native grounds. To hear such a scholar speak of the clash of Amr's three thousand Arab invaders with the sedentary Christian husbandmen who until the seventh century had had the northern Nile to themselves is to see his eyes flash. His face lights wistfully, as if he yearns to have been there too.

Lovers of myths and bravery, these foreign Arabists, after years of championing the underdog, as they believed, and feeling all but unrepresented in the American press (the bitterest among them speak of Israel as "Disneyland"), see their side beginning to surge. Neither in Egypt nor in Israel did I run across anybody who indicated much understanding of the human claims of the other country. The Egyptians' response to mention of the Nazi inferno is (brusquely) that while Westerners may consider it to be the great tragedy of Western civilization since slavery, it had nothing to do with Arab society, and Arabs, not Westerners, have been expected to pay for it. Israelis, for their part, because Zionism and the Balfour Declaration preceded the Holocaust, will often claim that guilt over the Holocaust has had no bearing on the West's support for Israel, that fury over the Holocaust, redirected, has not fired the vivid, uncompromising zeal with which Israelis battle the Arabs.

The Israelis properly complain that unexceptionable standards of international behavior are expected of them and of no one else. The Arabs rightly complain that among the major powers there has been a school of thought that has welcomed a feisty Israel in their midst to whittle away at their capacity to attain economic independence. The Arabs have indeed been the underdogs, but this is gradually changing, and because the Israelis, too, expect an enlightened sort of conduct from themselves, the nuclear punch they have been hoarding up seems somehow unconvincing: a holocaust visited upon peasant peoples by the survivors of a holocaust. What the Israelis declare privately, when you ask where their hopes are fixed, is that as the Arabs gain the technology that will enable them to destroy Israel someday, they themselves will be altered in ways that will make them not aim for that. Along with the technological sophistication may come a "post-Koranic tolerance."

"Nobody likes a dictatorship," an Egyptian official told me wearily. His countrymen found the Soviets' governmental system nearly as unappetizing as their atheism—found them stolid personally, miserly as tourists (interested only in purchasing gold), and were driven to distraction by the Soviet practice of renegotiating any contract when the matter of spare parts came up. Compared with Morocco, Libya, the Shah's Iran, or the several European dictatorships that first defined the term, Egypt is not now a "police state." The ordinary citizen is no more afraid of the ordinary police than in a democracy, and the activities of the plainclothes police have been shrinking, not expanding. Through the three "forums" of the Arab Socialist Union party—right, center, and left, each with some representation in the press — a path is being prepared for differing candidates to compete, to a limited extent, for seats in the parliamentary Assembly.

When listening to the rhetoric from all sides in the Middle East, it is possible to be very pessimistic. But this is to say that Egypt—an ancient and poignant nation—is teetering both on the edge of an experiment with "post-Koranic" democracy and on the brink of famine and total catastrophe; and that it behooves us to wish her well, as we have not always done.

1976

THE RIDGE-SLOPE
FOX AND THE
KNIFE THROWER

Saturday. I've finally fiixed the
waterline and got the hot-water heater working and so will
take a bath to mark the evening, although it's worth noting
how many other treats of one sort or another I have at my
disposal: wine, beer, vodka, whiskey, coffee, chocolate for
cocoa, maple syrup, honey, jam, apple cider, just for start-
ers. The pioneer whose cellar hole in the bramble patch I
dig in occasionally for Castoria bottles and other curios
might have had only a little sugar for his nightly tea and
maybe a spare ounce of vanilla to spike his spring water for
solace. He was a logger, down from New Brunswick, to
judge from the lettering on the chemists' bottles, and had
no lemon juice, no freeze-dried cubes of chicken broth or
lamb tongues in Australian aspic to pique his palate. It is
sometimes announced nowadays that we are becoming
more and more specialized individually, because of the increasing specialization of the professions, but on the con-

trary, we are all becoming generalists—almost protean. We have the leisure for it; or if we like our work, our work may take us all over.

My dog outdoors is a sentinel in case somebody drives up from the highway, a rather formidable route until the road commissioner makes his yearly pass with the grader—although of course, contrary to appearances, I *want* someone to come. Loneliness is my middle name just at the moment. Having driven for eight hours from the city in order to be alone, I'm "dying" of loneliness; can't seem to live with people or live without them. Lovers in comedies shout at each other, "I'll never speak to you again!" and the most abbreviated bout of lovemaking is much more cheering than masturbation. This need we have to talk continually, to rub or at least bump shoulders, is of substantial significance. An anthropologist might claim that the habit of keeping company has been graven into us as social creatures as a survival mechanism and isn't in some sense a matter of immortality—soul next to soul. Perhaps, indeed, it isn't, but the fascination is that it *might be.*

A New York City editor has asked me for an article about "the invigorating effects of silence," and yet I sometimes find silence enervating, and play the radio so much I fall asleep with it still playing. These cutover New England woods are bilingual when they do speak, as when one stumbles over an ancient scrap of reddish barbed wire bound around a line of pasture birches now lost in a new wilderness of outlaw growth. The sugaring trails are all but effaced, and isolated, suffering apple trees, bloomless lately, are slowly strangling to death in what was once a farmer's water meadow but has become an alder swamp. Some coyotes and a bounding white wolf-sized wild dog live here in

86

this brief interval between the rival epochs of farming and of summer-home development.

In the silence in the house one hears the drumming-ticking of the stove and an ovenbird's or veery's song. The wind sounds like the brook and the brook like the wind, though from the way the dog tilts his head I can infer the presence of a deer in the clump of poplars below the house. It would all be very well, except that the birds give their best voice at dawn and the deer—a barren doe whose fortunes I have followed for years (she is lonely herself)— only comes down off my neighbor's land to mine to feed at 6:00 P.M., which leaves a lot of time to kill, and I'm a city man and life is short to me.

City people try to buy time as a rule, when they can, whereas country people are prepared to kill time, although both try to cherish in their mind's eye the notion of a better life ahead. Country people do not behave as if they think life is short; they live on the principle that it is long, and savor variations of the kind best appreciated if most days are the same. City people crowd life when they have the chance; and it is nonsense to suppose that they have become "less observant," less alert than old-time country people were. Even that pioneer, whose lumpy, sharp-roofed log house I have a photo of, and who listened each morning for the location of his big neighbor, the bear, was not more on his toes than the Los Angeles denizens who, four abreast and tailgating, drive the Santa Monica Freeway at seventy miles an hour. His hearing and eyesight may have been better, but the city dweller, it should be borne in mind, wears out his eyes and ears from encountering so much so fast.

Country people tend to consider that they have a corner on righteousness and to distrust most manifestations of cleverness, while people in the city are leery of righteousness but ascribe to themselves all manner of cleverness. The countryman in the meantime, however—at least in my experience—drops in his tracks from a coronary just as promptly and endures his full share of ulcers and nervous attacks, so that his famous procrastination, which is as characteristic a tendency as his righteousness, does him little concrete good. Whether it's the local lawyer you have business with, or the carpenter, the highway engineer, a nearby farmer with a tractor, the delays almost defy belief. Conventionally, most of us, both in the city and the country, say, "Oh, they enjoy life more upstate, and so naturally they work slower." More often, instead of that, it's the undifferentiated outlook they take toward work. Not that there is some fuzzy idea abroad in the country that every farmer is as good as any other farmer. But a cow is finally just a cow, a chore is after all a chore, there is small possibility of what is called in the city "advancement," and so many hard chores remain to be performed in a long lifetime that, even allowing for the satisfactions of craftsmanship, if you keep putting some of them off, you may get away with having to do fewer of them in the end.

What the countryman does frequently possess is a face more content with middle age; and this is an important phenomenon to try to understand, because one of the central questions—central in the sense that if we could ever answer it we'd know a lot—is why our faces lose so much of the hopefulness apparent in photographs taken around the age of nineteen. On our deathbed, in the last throes of death, a strangely convinced, calm, smiling hopefulness will capture our faces once again, if we are like most people, displacing the anxiety and pain that had been there and astonishing the relatives left behind. But in between, why is it "heartbreaking," as both my wife and mother like to say, to look at somebody's picture from a time when he or she was young instead of middle-aged? It scarcely matters who is pictured; a sorrowful, protective feeling sweeps over us as we look at his face then: "Little did he know."

The sag, the defeatism of the mouth, the callused look about the eyes are not merely an instance of tissue wear and tear, and because older people in the country wear the same expressions that city people do when they get old, it may be that country folk, leading a life of less density, simply require longer to reach a similar point. Certainly the tenacity of grudges here in the country would indicate that life is slower rather than necessarily happier. My insurance agent hasn't said a pleasant word to me for six years because of a tiff we had, whereas no city man in his right mind would expend such a supply of bile on a single small affair; he'd have too many in hand. The finality of feuds implies a finality to life's possibilities too: a barn tying sixty-five cattle, one hundred thirty-five acres in pasturage and hay, a muddling spouse, four chubby children, seven good friendships, and three keen feuds.

But this analysis leaves out the sweetness of the mornings here, the mists swirling above the pond, the whap of a beaver's tail as you walk by, and what the postman means when he says he's "a rabbit hunter and a horned-pout fisherman." He means that he's not after bear or salmon; and he turned down the postmaster's job a couple of years ago for good measure, so that they had to bring in an outsider. Your true city man and countryman have become rare birds, in any case. Mostly now it's shopping malls, and the confusion is compounded by the fact that with the fanaticism of the convert, some of the most determined urbanites are really country boys who have fled from their boyhoods in the country, and many an overalled bumpkin maneuvering a Rototiller is chewing up two or three decades of city memories as he goes.

I get out of my car after the drive of eight hours, unbutton my fly, and piss on the lawn with a rich complex of feelings. The raccoons that very night take note that I have regained possession. In the country you know when your neighbor wakes up in the morning because smoke starts to waft up from his chimney. And we will always have that —those who want it. The mountain I look up at is late Devonian, when the amphibians were making news. Up top live black-poll warblers and golden-crowned kinglets that would fit the stunted spruces of a timberline more to the north or else much higher, and I am proud we have them. Still, the silence preys on me at times like noise, with the difference only that noise in its destructive impact is physiological and silence is harmless until the mind exfoliates ogres from it. Silence is exhilarating at first—as noise is— but there is a sweetness to silence outlasting exhilaration, akin to the sweetness of listening and the velvet of sleep. Particularly listening, because we listen for what we live for, which is to say, love and the peace of love and spontaneous joy. Maybe they never materialize, but the wood thrush's fluty cry, the hiss of the Coleman lantern at night are bridges of the sort that get us by meanwhile. It delights me to realize that right now a brown trout is filling her white belly with mosquitoes a mile down the road, that the glossy black sow bear who lives across the way has produced her biennial pair of cubs, to judge by the prints in the mud. At some point in the summer I'll put them up a tree and hear their peacock cries to her and her angry chuffing at me. Like the doe, she comes down to my bog to feed and I'm happy to pay the taxes on it so that, in this day and age, she can.

I'm surrounded by hatchlings—have scouted up the grouse that produces chicks each spring at the head of the upper field, to count how many she has: three black-brown feather-fluffs with needly beaks frozen as straight as ships in the short grass to deceive me. Two ravens have a nest on the cliff, around where the sunrise hits, and the pair of hawks whose presence I have enjoyed for years have safely returned, prudent in relation to a human figure on the ground. In incongruous mews and squeals they chat back and forth as they sail and soar. The hummingbirds, the bats, the man-prints of porcupines and coons—all as before, except that the bad winter appears to have cut into the population of bats. On the oak trees and striped maples flower tassels hang from the twigs; daffodils and shadbush blooms have given place to trillium, ground phlox, and cherry blossoms. I may miss seeing the ridge-slope fox, but glimpsed him last year with a tattered chipmunk drooping like a cigar from his mouth, tired and angling toward home, so I know where he lives. The white wolf-dog I've already caught sight of—watching me and watching his feet, he organized his escape plan as he fled—and my square house with its steep roof like a hat pulled low over the eyes: sometimes I would gladly drive for fifty hours to have these things.

The snow, which as a summer person I am content to miss, as not the least of its services, muffles the egos of people hereabouts, so that New Englanders are easier to swallow than a good many Californians or Texans (although the heat of the Deep South can do the same). The winter squats on them, much as the abrasions of city living are likely to moderate a person's self-esteem, not to rule him entirely but to keep him down to scale. Unfortunately, the snowfall can be so intimidating that it overly humbles people and turns them punch-drunk by the time spring comes. Besides, the tradition of self-deprecation has been institutionalized in New England to the point of absurdity. It's a relief in the autumn to get back to the smart-mouths of the city.

Of course my own "snowfall" at the moment is this upsurge of loneliness, in which a failure is implied: failure, to begin with, because one must dodge off to a solitary refuge. We like to blame the need for second homes on society, saying that our cities are unlivable, but the failure is personal, first of all. Alone at last, with the trees bulging above us in shapes that have defined and preserved the world, we find that we're incapacitated for living alone also.

Solitude is not a plaything. A friend of mine who is a professional explorer describes the violent seizures that have overwhelmed him on occasion—an irresistible shaking lasting for a couple of hours during which his body gradually fought off a nervous collapse. He lay in his tent, hugging himself and moaning, his best hope to give way to it until it stopped. These episodes have occurred not when he was absolutely by himself but, rather, when he was traveling with three or four morose and badly assorted companions, all of them hunkering around a greasy fire, rubbing soot off their biscuits, each hoarding a cup of smoky soup and facing in a different direction. Another veteran traveler has described for me the set of routines by which he wards off hysteria. Lunch is a production if possible, as a matter of habit; and then a nap; cocktails at five; note-taking during the morning; his diary in the evening—a fuss to record everything. Talk to your seatmate on the cross-Maharashtra bus—meals are always made much of—and in every city never refuse a gambit. *"Psst. Hey, mister,"* whispers a dragoman—go with him! He finds he gets a second wind; the loneliness strikes in several sieges, and to weather one means a respite, a spate of pleasures, before the next.

Both men are still fascinated, as I am, to speculate on what would happen if they were left on their own for many months. How soon and in what manner would they go mad? The wildlife biologists who are most inspired and acute turn out to be such isolated souls when one meets them in civilized surroundings that for them the seclusion of snow-leopard country in the Karakoram Range is hardly a departure. I know another individual (these people interest me) who, unlike the rest of us, doesn't worry that he might come unstrung in a situation of ultimate solitude. He has discovered that in the practical world there is no such circumstance. It is his pleasure—when he has saved a few thousand dollars—to land himself at the north rim of the Sahara with a strapped suitcase in one hand and a windbreaker in the other and wait for his first ride.

Unannounced, with no expedition behind him, he will step from a pirogue onto the coast of one of the outer islands of Indonesia and see what happens. What does happen—either there, or back behind the wall of the Andes, or in Kurdistan—is that within several hours he is not alone; he is with a tribesman, then fifteen tribesmen, and the story continues familiarly. He has special qualities. He is a linguist, a sexual switch-hitter, and possessed of a sliding, enigmatic smile and the gift of equanimity in equal measure with his fearlessness, and, like the other two, is an Olympic athlete at feats of solitude compared to you and me.

In Africa I've had my handwriting disintegrate at a border crossing from a case of bad nerves, so that I couldn't cash a traveler's check and was almost barred entry on grounds of illegibility. Even in these modest woods, loneliness muffles me like snow, and my sad penis at night, like a club in my hand—futile as a club, and a Stone Age implement for all of us, which is why we love it so—reminds me of many failings stretching far afield from sex. It is our saving grace that despite every social and scientific innovation and all our cumulative monkeying, if a man lays hands on a woman of his choosing and doesn't feel his penis swell with blood, his life can still be altered catastrophically. Though such is not my trouble, it's out here, holding this stubborn, thick appendage—never more impotent than when hard—that the relativism of the city appears in its full foolishness: the idea that anything goes.

The perception that our individual anguish is part of a tide of anguish and our exuberance part of a wave of joy is a religious one. We are all fragile—the health-food faddist down the road, throwing up his health foods now and submitting to anesthetic injections in the last stages of cancer; the counterculture young folk in the town knotting their brows at meetings of the Low Income Association, figuring how they, too, can become a clubhouse pressure group.

I went through a siege of cancer with a friend, and one of the spectacles that took shape in her mind as she waited between operations was an inspection of the raggle-taggle file of admirers with whom she'd shared a span of twenty years. No rosy glasses now: each was the subject of some hilarity, because trysts—just as in Chaucer—keep more kindly in the memory if treated as a stumble. As a Jewish intellectual, she had been lured by ethnic opposites or seamen, movers, actors, not seeking a mirror of herself but what she didn't already have, so that an obvious unconformity recurred. They weren't unlike a row of knotty "problems" as she ranged them up, trying to draw some conclusions. She could claim that she had left each of them a little better off than when she'd met him—his career clarified, perhaps, if he had one, his nervous system temporarily rehabilitated. To her surprise, the lover with the longest tenure had dwindled almost to a cipher in her recollection. Instead, her favorite was a motorcycling German who had joked with her and put her in the hospital and whom she hadn't taken seriously. At supper parties with his pals, she'd used to reach up her left sleeve and with a flourish remove her bra—but now girls had stopped wearing bras. Her former husband she had married on the rebound from another man, a man whom she herself had turned away, she realized, although he'd loved her endlessly and though indeed she may have loved him more than her husband. For having seemed to love her too much, at last he'd had to marry someone else. She remembered being told as a little girl by her aunt—the beauty in the family, whom she was thought to take after—to marry someone who loved her not only more than all the world but more than she loved him; and so she'd done the opposite.

Once I read about a medieval death imposed by a potentate on two lovers. He had their arms tied around each other and left them lying face-to-face to starve. Supposedly the horror of it was that they would grow to loathe each other, sweating in this mockery of the coital position, but I don't see it so; I remember my explorer friend shivering, hugging his ribs in a tent in New Guinea. Recently two revolutionaries were hanged in the Near East, and as they twisted, blindfolded, their hands tied behind their backs happened to touch, and touching, clasped, and so they died grasping each other.

Everything is so fragilely a matter of interpretation that we tread on the edge of mayhem or suicide if a tilt occurs in our minds. Sex and laughter were the original belly-pokers, and with inhibition came civilization, but there is such significance to loneliness that we still continue to suffer from it; we can't exist complacently, puttering about, watching TV, and sleeping, but instead are pulled together with an urgency, as if, apart, we had no skins. When it sets in, it springs up again although well placated only the day before: an awful ache, and what it partly is—as the anthropologists would agree—is the call of the wild, as one looks down at one's funny legs, which in their quirky shape have more to do with trotting across a grassy valley in company with a hunting party than accelerating a car. In the city, I live overlooking an elevated highway and can hear around the clock a rush of traffic, most of which cannot be going anywhere terribly exciting, but pressing, pressing, just the same. Once when the highway was out of commission it rapidly became populated with joggers, who also traveled up and down.

I don't stay still either, and give people that traveler's "Bye-bye" when I leave, though afterwards when I am under way I worry that I'm smashing up my life by my avoidances and indecisions. A friend who is seventy-nine, the only person hereabouts interested enough in scouting in the woods to pinpoint a den of coyotes that everyone was speculating about, whisks his hand lightly over his bald head to betoken the speeding years—says they go by for him like slices falling from a loaf of bread. He was born in his own bedroom, but never having left Vermont, he's brought the world to him. That is, he regularly sees in his woodlot "tigers," "moose," "mountain lions."

I keep a turtle for the same reason. He hasn't surrendered to being a pet, and pauses in his escape attempts only long enough to eat a mouthful of strawberries. He may be as old as I am, to judge by the rings on his scutes, and as an experienced campaigner he knows that the hard knocks of captivity are not to be accepted as anything but temporary. I keep him in the rabbits' pen to confirm that, as in the fable, he covers much more ground than they do. To look at him, it wouldn't seem he could; and just as unexpectedly, his dogged efforts to escape—banging down on his back from halfway up the fence—are gradually accomplishing exactly what he seeks. I'm moved by his persistence and will soon release him. He looks like a brown chock of wood, and has a thumb-shaped head and mail-like, horny plates of armor on the front of his wide legs to shield them when he draws them inside his shell. But when he opens himself again—stretching out his legs and head—behind the head and sleeves of mail protecting his legs are a tender pair of shoulders, puffy with the fat that he has put on between escape attempts. Both these, and certain dashings on the previously hidden portions of his legs, are a passionate orange.

He lives under a roof of brown bone, on a hard bedboard, carrying his bed about with him, using it as a fifth leg in many of his maneuvers, as when he slides down off a log. He sleeps with his hind legs lolled out personably and his head poignantly at rest. His fire-colored shoulders must identify him to other turtles of the species, and it was probably his search for a mate that brought him out to the dirt road where I caught him. Otherwise he is remarkably footloose, has no social life to speak of (the rabbits are more interested in making friends with him), and seems almost as free from any knowledge of the pangs of hunger as of loneliness. He needs to be plump enough to survive hibernation, but shouldn't get so fat that his limbs can't pull wholly into his shell if a raccoon should happen to grab him and begin to scratch and gnaw.

Because turtles are willing to starve in captivity, their usual form of surrender is only to agree to eat. But his manner of pausing for a worm, casually letting the crumbs of it fall from the corners of his mouth as he continues to search for a hole in the fence, makes him seem more of a figure to me than merely fatalistic resistance by starvation would. Certainly his singular shell must have saved his life when he has been caught by human beings—as well as raccoons—before. For every dozen people who will immediately stomp on a snake, only one will want to kill a turtle.

He pumps his throat as he breathes, in an exercise reminiscent of cud-chewing, and expresses contentment by this, as dogs by the sounds of their breathing express affection to one another and to us. Even on his back after a fall, he rests, not panicked, because his mastery of the uses of his shell is like a hockey player's with a stick. He sometimes talks to himself with the thump of it, I think—employing or not employing the sound, choosing or not choosing to thump —and, like the elegant fire-flickerings of his shoulders and legs, it is a more eloquent statement than his official hiss.

A Friday, later.

I have a friend or two whose only response to adversity is to retreat to this same harshness of the woods to cauterize a failure or a wound. They buckle themselves into it like putting on ice packs. No doubt, like me, they go into the woods to celebrate also—the astounded feeling that you get from looking at a tadpole balancing in the water with his large tail, but sprouting four dark legs. Even a farmer hacking a path through a side of beef to stock his freezer is dismantling a structure of wonder and grace.

I cook rhubarb, nibble wood-sorrel, and steep the house with the smell of wild-meat roasts. Outward self-sufficiency, and yet I keep the radio on—women's voices from Canada announcing Schumann and speaking French. Whatever they are saying sounds loving to me.

In the past, when I have felt a divorce action drawing near, I've put a tent and sleeping bag in my car; a friend of mine sets a canoe on his truck—gestures about as germane as an Edwardian reserving a room at his club. But, sleeping bag and all, I am so lonely now that it is like a hemorrhage. Listening to the clicking noise of my dog licking his paws, feeding the stove past midnight till my hands sink and the knuckles get burned, I groan beastly groans or burst into loud phrases that might seem disconnected if they weren't embarrassingly transparent, with my belowstairs mind standing right in back of my tongue. A girl who lives as a squatter in a hut over the hill, when she gets into company where the talk is too much for her, makes a zipping motion across her temple to show that she has lost her way again. Chop-chop-chop she goes with her hips, in bed with the axmen who in payment will chop her winter's wood.

In midwinter the game warden, touring on his snowmobile, generally discovers somebody from the city still holed up in a cabin around here piled high with snow, a cashiered engineer from Boston, who used to work in aerospace but has denned up like a bear sucking on its toes and claws. The first woods travelers in America—men like Peter Kalm, William Bartram, and Crèvecoeur—appear from their journals to have been a peaceable lot who, in exploring the God-given world, didn't find it necessary to become entangled overmuch with aborigines, as would have been the case on one of the hotter continents. Mostly they met other whites—energetic, appreciative souls, on the whole, who shared their gaiety. Now we are likely to lie low with our energies instead of walking, and do it in order to take stock, which is what we busy ourselves with a good deal anyway. Although the country hideaway, set in a kind of tuning-fork relationship of tension to the city, where the owner's money or reputation is actually made, is a new *modus operandi*, it is impossible to calculate the end of the effects of the closing off of all that old, free operating space.

At performances of the sideshow in a circus that I used to work for as a boy, I'd watch the knife thrower, after he had thrown at his wife (who was also the circus nurse), go into the second segment of his act, which was—to put it bluntly—to whip a series of women. He didn't need to ask for volunteers; he was besieged by them. In slacks and pleated blouses, cashmere sweaters and pedal pushers, they wanted the sensation of a horsewhip wrapping roughly around them, laid on by a black-haired, muscular man—the whole experience of a sexual lashing except (because of his skill) the pain. For him, too—both as a knife thrower who avoided murdering anybody and in the whipping performance—to go through the motions was sufficient.

There is a monster in me that I keep at bay by such reflexes as, for example, in the city, crooning to my young daughter while dandling her, "Your daddy is a monster to his little girl, so cruel to her." The true love in the voice vitiates the words; and I remember my own father gripping my arms fiercely at queer, furious instants when I was small and had done nothing especially wrong. I realize now that he was choking down a violence that did not really relate to me, lest I be hurt. He read sadistic popular fiction on occasion and must have been astonished by these impulses, as we all are, an astonishment which, at the layman's level, the science of psychology has not diminished. "Why are you watching this woman being whipped?" an inquiring reporter might have asked us at the sideshow; and as long as his expression was serious and he approached us one by one, not trying to challenge us as a mob, we would have been utterly abashed, at a loss to explain even in our private minds.

It's just as well, unless one believes in the perfectibility of man. Besides, there is the complication that the wife of the woman-whipper climbed off the platform—after he had thrown his knives at her—and, in a perfectly unruffled, competent manner, she went behind the hippo's tank to attend to a cage hand who was lying in a pile of straw shaking with pneumonia. The husband did the same when he was needed, and often stopped a minute in the "whippings" he administered to ask her how the patient was doing, when she emerged—seemed to care more than most of the rest of us.

Diana, goddess of the woods, was chaste, but we who go into the woods nowadays are as likely to be kinky as chaste. Still waiting to get to sleep, with this shillelagh or grease gun in my fist (really like a little squirrel)—what to do with him?—I have a fantasy that at least has the virtue of logic. I am an itinerant slave dealer and toward the end of the day I have the women walk in front of my horse with their skirts pinned up so I can watch their buttocks swing and pick a partner for the evening. Other fantasies, however, have me harnessed to a cart, instead of playing the master; or where I wear a nose ring and am in bed attached to a woman's necklace, like a kind of living bauble. And however astutely you explain masochism, it is not logical.

Women after Diana have usually left men to their own devices in the woods, as perhaps we have wished. Nevertheless, we do people it; and the recent fantasies I've had depict me lying on my side on the bed with my hands tied behind my back and fastened to a ring around the base of my scrotum. Helpless but not in discomfort, I move about at times and am in use as a sort of dildo by an amused woman, closer to forty than thirty (I am identified as being "young"), who feeds me from her mouth or with her hands, first fastening me between her legs with my throat pressing against her so that she can feel me swallow. She releases me to exercise but keeps the intimacy tight between us, rationing my sexual activity.

I'm not unique in this variety of vision. The prostitutes are telling the sociologists that they are being inundated at the moment by men seeking extreme humiliation. Is it death the customers are really after? The woman of my fantasy —self-besotted, like the mannequin who stands in for me— does not resemble the women who in fact inhabit my memories. I do still yearn to be initiated, however, and try to manufacture opportunities for that in lovemaking. I'm boyish, as if only through boyishness can I slip through the woman's resistance to win her indulgence.

There are two ways for a man to be boyish, both corresponding to a woman's "flirtation." One of them simply reclaims the years of first courtship, salting those blundering forms of appeal with irony and directness—the haste of people who recognize that they are mortal—and strikes the rest of us as pleasing because the person seems to occupy all of his life at once. But the other boyishness is compulsive, like a child's dizziness in the environs of Mum. In his abject imaginings, the prostitute's client gropes backward, I suspect, and not forward towards death.

It is marriage as often as bachelorhood that creates "dirty old men," or, for that matter, their counterpart, the "biddy." The person's inversion grows as a stain from his defeats, retreats, dysfunctions, and the gap between what life supposedly held in store for him and what life brought.

Perhaps he gave himself over to his daydreams until the daydreams altered him, or found that his choice was between waking up in the same house with his children in the morning but living with a woman who would not sleep with him, or forlornly leaving them to go and live with somebody who would.

I used to ask the first girl I ever made love to to spread her legs as widely as she could and raise them high, as if to dramatize that the shut legs I had met with before had opened at last. But I have another memory, startling because it came back unannounced after a hiatus of many years. It's of my first wife, before our marriage, sleeping on the floor beside my bed—her bed, actually, narrow, in a narrow apartment—and the pretext was that there was just space for one. Such memories, a dozen or twenty of them, cast a greenish, unnerving light over one's past. I didn't need to drive so far, eat wild meat, live with a bat-faced dog, and burn kerosene in order to bump up against them, but here they stand in relief.

Only in a roundabout way are weeks spent in the wilderness "purifying," and then only when the affair is brought to a conclusion before the person is disabled. As in the old medical practice of leeching, the stamina has been bled out of me. I came here brim-up with city sarcasms and the woods soon overpowered these alkalis. If I stay on, as I've learned from experience, the woods will continue melting the edginess out of me, to a point of faith and glee and exultancy in the sailing foliage, the cut of the sunshine and rain —right on past this point of equilibrium, to my becoming runny butter on the ground. Arriving, I've had in me both the tigers that treed Black Sambo in the fairy tale and Black Sambo himself. The tigers run around and around these trees, to which, terrified, I cling, until they (the tigers) gradually melt, and chastened—meek as Sambo was—I climb down, and, tiptoeing through a puddle that was a tiger once, steal away to the city again.

I get a glimpse, in other words, of what must have happened a good many times on the frontier. That pioneer in his uneasy solitude, with his vial of vanilla extract and endless spring water, for periods of an hour or two every few days began to imagine he had a brass ring around his testicles that his hands were fastened to. He was seven miles from a neighbor, two days' walk from town, and by stages these spells extended to several hours, almost daily, the daydream evolving into a hallucination he could no longer control. Though in his own mind he wasn't alone at all, month by month it reached such a pass that he could hardly snatch time to hoe his potatoes or hunt for meat. Eventually, walking around with his hands clasped behind his back, he stopped splitting wood. The fire went out, and one freezing night, lying with his hands that way, he died.

This is my one life and what is kinky in me worries me less than the dead spots. Kinkiness, like a reversible coat, can be turned inside out. A vulnerability, innocent as well as in despair, is represented, which, even if the opposite side is no more appetizing, makes for some leeway.

I have a clipping from Dien Bien Phu that shows a French major standing on a little rise with his arm raised to his men, more in salutation than command. He is leaf-thin, sleepless, soon to die. His hands sag exhaustedly. Like a leaf, he is beginning to curl at the ends, though his smile and long arms still carry the greeting, which is larger than his body.

It's incongruous that the older we get, the more likely we

are to turn in the direction of religion. Less vivid and intense ourselves, closer to the grave, we begin to conceive of
ourselves as immortal. But if the presentiment is even half
correct, naturally, too, it would await our closer attention.
The sweetness of ordinary people's voices singing together
can be taken as evidence, for instance: the absolutely
unearthly beauty they acquire in combining with each
other, which has no relation to the honking quality each
voice is cursed with, alone. In an era of canned entertainment, we hear one hundred voices singing together nowadays mostly in church, but whatever the setting, if the
whole is so much greater than the parts, we might deduce
the existence of God.

"Once I realized I couldn't rescue myself, an indescrib-
able feeling of calmness and serenity came over me," a man
who had nearly drowned told two researchers from the University of Iowa. Interviewing more than a hundred survivors
of near-death situations, they discovered that a slowing of
external time "and a vast recall of happy events were generally linked and clearly related." Many people "described
their emotional state as pleasurable, and twenty-three percent even acknowledged joy."

The very root of my own hopefulness is a long stint I
spent working in an army morgue—the odd smiles of most
of the dead as death had overtaken them and the nature of
death had dawned on them. Or maybe, on the contrary, the
revelation was not really so much of death as of the nature
of life, as an extravaganza of glad scenes sped past their
eyes. Either way, a simple explanation referring to the vicis-
situdes of evolution would not do justice to the sense of
peace their expressions implied. We can argue that the reason women tend to forget the pain of childbirth is so that

105

they can consent to have more children, but an epiphany arising from the convulsions of death itself bears no such interpretation.

Recently I went to Europe for the first time in ten years, sailing at night; and for me, on board, the event was rife with premonitions of living forever, although, of course, death is also pictured as being some sort of shipping out. Many people get these feelings—smiling at their enemies as at their friends, all of us to meet someday in a theater removed. I was ten years older, noticeably frailer on deck in the wind, and yet the sensation was as sharp as a yelp, compounded partly of my happiness and the ship's floodlit angles and New York City's big straight stripe of lights, which were yellow and hospitable-looking, stippled softly across a thousand buildings—as if, for me, this were not one of perhaps a last handful of trips across the Atlantic but one of an infinite number of sailings.

Manhattan makes a handsome showing from the water, with its streets orange slashes and the parcels of dark warehousing adding bulk and contrast to the lighted skyscrapers and apartment complexes, until the Battery and World Trade Center finish the narrative with a concentrated statement of what power is. Then the green, puff-chested Statue of Liberty, crusted with fame, and the green-lighted East River bridges, as you look back. I was on the *Queen Elizabeth II* for the fun of the voyage, the memories of earlier sailings, and the notion that crossing between continents ought to be a momentous undertaking. I wanted to feel the earth move under me and to rattle across a rough roadbed, because lying in one's stateroom in a light sea is rather like a railroad journey. I wanted to know for five days that I was afloat on the ocean, hearing not just surf sounds—which are a translation—but the immensity of the original source. Eighteen thousand feet of water below, and the grip of it insisting that one is not going to put one's foot down just any old where, but *there*, and now over *there*, and now over *there*. "Crossing the pond," the sailors say, with their faces belying the words.

And so, shivers of anticipation as we got under way, although, still the New Boy in middle age, I bumbled twice to the dining room with my briefcase bumping against my knee, being sized up humorously by the British waiters, before ascertaining that I needn't forfeit my dinner to watch the sailing. There were English round-trippers ("Oh, have you just come aboard?"), and English who had flown to America only the day before. Also a young fan of British shipping from Tooting who had gone to visit the *Queen Mary* in her concrete slip in Long Beach, California, having paid for the jaunt by running a roller coaster in Santa Cruz; and a couple of nurses who had been slaving away in Fort Worth, imported with three hundred of their countrywomen to do a year of night duty. So many English don't like living in England, one meets them all over—English girls going out to Australia or veering around again.

In the rush on the pier I had kissed my daughter good-bye but had forgotten to kiss my wife and had tried to shout to her afterwards from the deck of the ship that I was sorry. Though, like most men, I have polygamous impulses, I don't generally try to "renew" myself by chasing after another generation of women—it is old friends I hanker after —and so after I had made a pass at one of the English nurses, I settled quite contentedly into the deck-chair society of other sedentary individuals. Even so, traveling is bound to be a polygamous experience, as one's memory works. My first wife and I had made a crossing, and she was here and would be again, I realized, in Orsini Castle, the Pitti Palace, and half a dozen other places. Both wives, with their poignant, slim necks—high collars—strolled the deck.

My father, too, was on the ship, because he'd always sailed off to an assignment in Europe on one of the Cunard *Queens* if he could. An exceedingly innocent man for a lawyer, he, like me, had been a little scared upon departure —you could see it in his back as he went up the gangplank —and sometimes did meet with adventures, such as returning to his hotel room in West Berlin to find four fishy fellows going through his luggage. His travels, like mine, were mostly alone, because my mother's romantic fancies led her elsewhere, but he was trusted on sight by most strangers, and I could envision him right now beginning the process of striking up new acquaintances. Abroad, he was bad at learning the language of the country—the words just couldn't seem to jack themselves together in his mouth— but on his feet he had a fast sense of direction. He was reasonably tolerant of foreign customs, considering his intolerance of ethnic variations at home, but feared the germs on foreign money and disliked handling foreign currency; liked to "crack" bills in a mannerism I found irritating. He had bowel troubles, which he regarded so solemnly that the rest of the family took his alarums as a joke. (Once he flew clear home from Switzerland because of a case of constipation.) Then, however, he contracted bowel cancer, mourning his feet as they swelled up and died before his eyes, mourning his legs likewise.

I am evasive with people who are gravely ill, and what I most regret with respect to my father is not so much that

secret hunchback residing in me who exulted to learn that
he was dying—because the psychological phenomenon of
sons set irremediably against their fathers is not something
we are responsible for—but, instead, the genuinely grieving
side that did wish urgently to help but miscalculated what
to do. Sometimes when he sought sympathy, instead of
mourning right along with him, I tried to "cheer him up." I
remember him looking down at his legs, which were mori-
bund and withering, and myself saying to him, "Oh, but
you still have your brain!"

Swaddled like a sanatorium patient in the deck chair,
drinking bouillon, chewing ship's biscuits, I couldn't fail to
think of his last couple of ocean cruises; it seemed to be
how he had wanted to go out of the world. Or maybe he'd
felt convinced—like me in the excitement of the ship's sailing—that he would live forever if he was on the sea. Rattling
along in a "ripple sea," with the broad band of white wake
behind, an unvarnished stream of brown smoke above the
ship in bright sunshine, and the vigorous longboats overhead as you paced the boat deck, it surely did appear as
though, if God in the thrust of his vivacity were not be-
nign, there must be multiple gods, because *one* of them was.

In a "moderate" sea, with thumps in it, knocking against
three sides of the cabin, and the hull of the ship stretching
and creaking, I had headaches and a weighty stomach, but
this was part of what I'd come for. The steward kept four
canaries, which he let fly in the corridor at night. He spoke
of the ship as "goldier" than either the true-blue old *Q.E.*1
—which had just burned in Singapore—or the *Queen
Mary*. Both had had portholes that opened, instead of air
conditioning, so that a breeze blew through, and oak rather
than plastic and alloy paneling. The two ships used to ar-

range to salute each other visually in the mid–North Atlantic, a ceremony I had witnessed from the *Mary* one morning. Indeed, to be "a good sailor" was socially important in my parents' day.

For entertainment in the Double Room, a silver-painted puppet danced from the strings of a taller puppet, clothed in red, which was worked by a green-suited puppeteer with wooden movements and a frigid grin—until he suddenly finished and bowed fluidly, a human being again. A few hours out of New York, I had woken with a nightmare from the whirling of Nantucket Light, but by the landfall off Cherbourg the city's tics had drained from my face and the ocean's surge had engendered in me the illusion of a whole family history of involvement with it. The sea is also a crocodile—in the agony of swallowing water overboard—but I was on the ship. I rocked ashore, myself.

There are places in Ethiopia so high and silent that the villagers can listen to the wings of migrating birds miles away. They are roofless in the world, as we are too, if we remembered it. Digging earthworms for my turtle, sometimes I get the idea that nothing is more fleshly than worms are. Nutritionally, they are a quintessence of protein, and as white as one's secret flesh under one's pants. They are the flesh that fishermen root out before they go to try to catch a fish—and flesh is everything. To slide one's hand inside a lover's clothes is to want to leave it there forever—the buttocks larger than the hand. Life is at its sweetest when we have other flesh in hand besides our own. Vegetarians have often gone through some type of self-destructive phase before renouncing meat and are cleansing themselves, but we meat eaters eat to augment what we have, and, embracing, feast upon each other in order to amplify ourselves.

If human nature eventually is going to take the place of nature everywhere, those of us who have been naturalists will have to transpose the faith in nature which is inherent in the profession to a faith in man—if necessary, man alone in the world. It is not an impossible leap. I pick the sticks to cook my supper with, a ritual of intimacy with the fire and the wood, like my dog's delight in observing the chipmunks that he stalks. Like my handling a steak, there's nothing in his attentiveness toward what he hunts suggesting hate. Just now, I'm burning spruce floorboards torn up six years ago. Floorboards, like new birch logs, are made of sunshine too.

Outside, orange day lilies are in bloom, blue cornflowers, pink queen-of-the-prairie, rose-colored mallow, purple blossoms on the vetch, baby green apples, and red raspberries. On and on through the succession of quiet towns, the road from New York City seemed ready to lead me clear north to the Arctic if I kept driving. And yet I'm ready to retrace my steps awhile. City humor is expansive, New England's understated; New England humor is ironic, and the city's more festive. I want to sit down with some horse players again.

Country people believe they live close to the bone, close to the permanences, which, in the sense that nothing could be more evanescent than work accomplished in the country, they do. Their houses molder very promptly when unlived in. Their barns go broken-backed under the weight of the snow. Their fields quickly begin reverting to woods if left unmowed for more than three years in a row. Around here the most permanent work of inscription has been done by the bears on the beech trees.

Beeches possess a smooth, grayish bark, almost watercolored, which cuts as easily as the bark of paper birch, but doesn't peel as birch bark does. These were the trees that lovers carved their initials on back in the days when lovers knew the properties of different trees. The beech's skin, as tender as it is, will keep its scars right into old age, which may mean fifty or one hundred years or more, longer than the occupants of any house in this township will be remembered, even if the house continues to stand. In my junk woods of what the loggers call "widowmaker" stubs careening overhead and "schoolmarm" trees crotched so that no logger has wanted them, the marks of my friend the sow's climbs will outlive not only her own passions but mine.

The bears' favorite food in the early fall has been jewelweed, which is an orange-flowered, succulent herb that grows in clumpish profusion in wet soil until killed by the first hard frost. The same October frost will bring down heaps of small, triangular, thin-shelled beechnuts in spiny, little open burrs that the bears dote on. The pioneers used to spread blankets on the ground to catch the nuts, from which they made beech coffee, as well as a first-rate salad oil and a cooking flavoring whose faint echo we taste in beechnut chewing gum. So far, beech is not a wood much in demand by the timber industry, and the bears, having the trees to themselves, and feeling impatient and proprietary, will climb sixty or eighty feet into the crown of the fall foliage to shake the limbs and hurry the harvest along. In doing so, they leave a ladderlike series of neat claw prints going up (going down, the bear will slide as if the tree were a firehouse pole), incised with a particular fingering that manages to create a personal image of the bear involved that, for anybody who visits here a half-century from now, will have outlasted the memory of Vermont's present governor or Gerald Ford.

These ladders up the beech trees have a logic to them and are precious for that. The bears are manlike and their marks manlike, and so carry an authority and resonance because they reach way back and yet one can ride forward on the memory of them for a good while.

1976

BEING BETWEEN
BOOKS

There is the sense a writer has after finishing a book that he may have run out of words—have used up all the words that he is familiar with. Though perhaps he's full of ideas for his next book, he is likely to waffle a bit before beginning again until he feels his strength come back, so he won't make a botch of the first draft and vitiate some precious part of his enthusiasm in a false start. Instead, he busies himself with half-speed research of a kind, does book reviews or what are called "pieces" for magazines, travels, drinks, looks out for love affairs, or whatever.

If he is not a formula writer, he asks himself, *What shall I do with the rest of my life?* It is a privileged question, which practitioners in another profession might have to burn their bridges to ask. But a writer must really attempt to start from scratch and reach for new preoccupations, if he is not to rehash his earlier books. He does still like to look at them in their fading dust jackets on the shelf—that proud foot or so of space (which he has tried to extend with reprint editions), each inch of which represents a year or more of his life. If he is like most writers, his pleasure as he contemplates them is sad as well as sweet, because to actually open one and read what he wrote then is uncomfortable at best. He is pained he didn't write better, pained at how much of his original vision of each book he left out or was inadequately talented to convey to the page, and at how commonplace or insufficient even his first conceptions were. Yet he realizes too (at least if he has had some success along the way) that this disillusion is exaggerated and has the healthy purpose of making him work as hard as ever the next time to keep on trying to put things down that he had never thought to say before. His freedom—*What shall I do with the rest of my life?*—is arduous as much as enviable, though he will probably keep his mouth shut about his doubts about his work, lest somebody fail to disagree. Certainly, if he participates in the current vogue for plugging one's own volumes on television tours and campus junkets, he keeps mum, but at the cost of a good many pangs of irony, since he knows that the dissatisfaction he is concealing is a healthy, healing phenomenon and that the complacent sort of attitude that he implies during public appearances would not be.

So—new ground, new experiences, new kinds of people. Sometimes his hopes ride high that he can do it. Time is short. By covering his ears with his forearms he hears the roar of his own living body, and, by touching the hollows of his cheeks, foresees the feel of his dead skull. The mother of a writer friend of mine was a professional fortune-teller and crowned one particularly bitter family argument by informing her that her opinions on several subjects hardly mattered, anyway, because she was going to die between the ages of twenty-nine and thirty-two, which was a prediction wonderfully concentrating.

Writers come to recognize, however, that they will never manage an entirely fresh start, that they are limited by inescapable patterns, and, indeed, ought to be, if their work as a whole is to have coherence. Like it or not, they have to expect to repeat themselves—and here I take myself as an example. The boy who hitchhiked off at eighteen to join the Ringling Bros. Circus and write a novel about it, twenty-five years later "parachuted" into central Africa to get material for a book about doing that. Once again, after a little respite, the writer acquires the gaze of an assessor: *Can I use you?* His less favorite relatives, and other people who meet him and are not impressed, are inclined to wonder at how little interested in them, "for a writer," he seems. But his second concern—besides discovering what he needs to dip into among the million stories walking the streets— is what he doesn't need, or perhaps couldn't handle if he tried, which is the same.

Writers are bellyachers and self-dramatists, and complain a lot during the months preceding publication day. Their envy of one another, which fluctuates like a fever chart throughout their professional lives, goes up and down at a faster rate. One morning, anticipating a great reception for themselves, they overflow with magnanimity, and the next, mingy of spirit, will be unable to read any review friendly to someone else, a condition doubly ignoble when they have lost even enough sense of humor to understand what has happened to them. Many older writers reach the point where they have trouble reading, let alone praising, a successful book by a contemporary, though they may try to make up for it with a busy show of kindness toward younger writers, by "reevaluating" neglected figures, or championing writers persecuted in the Communist bloc. They are also likely to overpraise a particular kaffeeklatsch of aging, careworn pals, fearing, naturally, that in any general deflation of overblown reputations their own might pop. I have never met a writer who didn't suffer from jealousy, but in the unblanched youngster it is not yet a vice so bilious. He can interpret another's triumph as an omen for himself.

The more generous souls, like nice guys in other fields, don't usually finish either first or last. They finish in the middle and, like other middle-roaders, occasionally in midlife will seek a change of venue. That is, an essayist, for instance, is like an infielder in baseball. He performs a lot, making the pretty throw to first, punching the ball for some of his hits, but gradually he'll begin to yearn to range along the outfield fence. A novelist, on the other hand, appearing less frequently, striking out more often, as long-ball hitters do, if he tires of it, may begin to want to play third base.

But it's too easy to make fun of writers' occupational plaints, when, after all, unless they write from the fortress of a tenured professorship, they live without pension protection, a salary check or unemployment insurance, as insecurely as a rodeo cowboy—win or starve. Just as for anybody else, the toll that middle age exacts is measured in tiny blood specks in the eye and a pressurized or softened look about the head, as of an overripened cantaloupe. The novelist screws up his courage in order to invest another two or three years in another attempt to float a boat of original design upon an invented ocean. The risks involve a leap of empathy and, possibly, technical innovations as well. A journalist, being more strictly a documentor, may undertake an actual physical gamble as he pursues his idea for a book that neither he nor anyone else has quite grabbed hold of before. His eyes, ears, and nose have dimmed; also, incidentally, his sixth sense, if he used to have one, and other, more mundane manifestations of intuition. On the other hand, his understanding of people—the accuracy of his expectations—has probably increased. In middle age a novelist or journalist may not be as good at absorbing the raw material for his new books but is craftier at sorting through and emphasizing or staging the scene when he finally presents what he has learned. His successes have a different character and are achieved at the expense of charley horses he would not have experienced as a limber young man. In theory, he knows how to do almost everything a little better, but the question is whether he still has the wherewithal to carry out his plans.

A writer's thirties are often his best decade (*Moby Dick*). But one has also heard good things about the forties (*Huckleberry Finn*). Then come the fifties (*Don Quixote*), and, for brave people, even on beyond (Sophocles, Victor Hugo, Thomas Hardy, Thomas Mann). If he sells well and writes fast, our sample writer likes to remember that so did Dickens, in order not to feel that he is just potboiling. But if he is the opposite type, he thinks of the array of great writers, from Thoreau to Kafka, who did not write quickly and sell. In either case, as with the issue of aging, he knows that he is whistling in the dark in making any such comparison—that endless thousands of absolutely awful writers have comforted themselves by doing the same.

What he does possess, as a free-lance writer, is both his freedom and a lance. He knows the reason he doesn't write short stories as good as Chekhov's is simply that he doesn't write so well. Not that he lives in the wrong century or society, not that his politics or education is wrong. The limits placed on him are solely within himself, and so he knows that as long as he lives in decent health, a chance exists that he may break past those old limits to new capacities, that a book will seize his imagination that nobody on earth has yet conceived of, and that his tongue will finally be able to speak freely, as never before.

1979

AFRICAN
RAMBLE

Kenya has fourteen million people, whose per capita yearly income is $169, and no compulsory education (a fee of some sort is generally charged). Laborers in Nairobi earn about a dollar a day; those in agriculture, half a dollar. Less than 10 percent of the rural people have available an adequate water supply. More than a quarter of the nation's children suffer from some form of malnutrition, according to a World Bank report, and the population is expected to double in the next twenty-five years.

It's a country astride the equator on the Indian Ocean, but mostly semiarid, uncommonly beautiful, with views of the two highest mountains in Africa and so much else in the way of variety that although it's by no means large as African countries go, it seems grand and large. Except on the coast and in the Kikuyu, formerly "White," highlands, the look of the place to an American much resembles the redlands of New Mexico or the wide plains of Oklahoma forty years ago—New Mexico, that is, with elephants, and the Oklahoma of the dust bowl. To a drastic degree the country is blowing away through deforestation, from charcoal burning, slash-and-burn farming, and even the hungry foraging of the elephants, which, since the recent drought, find their grass gone. In 1975 the Kenya Game Department estimated a hundred and thirty thousand elephants remained in the country, only a third of which lived within the 5 percent of the land that had been gazetted as game reserve. Probably a thousand of these have been poached for their ivory each month since—ivory worth forty-five dollars a pound.

East Africa, it's said, is where tourists go who like animals better than (black) people. Less vividly, ethnically "African" than some of the nations on the west coast—and only one-fifth as populous as Nigeria, for instance—Kenya seems less formidably foreign. About forty thousand white residents have remained, exerting a considerable influence for efficiency in the give-and-take of the capital, and eighty thousand "Asians" of Indian or Pakistani origin still constitute the mercantile class. The passover of the great coffee and tea plantations (in Isak Dinesen's day Africans were not allowed to own land) has been gradual, financed by British government grants. Enough compensation is paid that the white farmers can retire quietly to the coral beaches of Mombasa and Malindi on the coast, if they please. Nevertheless, several hundred thousand good acres are still farmed by individual whites, not to mention the corporate pineapple and sisal and cotton plantations and beef ranches one runs into here and about. In a country where malnutrition is rampant, where close to 90 percent of the land is scarcely arable, or not arable at all, the white apple growers of Kitale still bury part of their crop to keep the price up. Nairobi is a city with fine restaurants, and beggars stretched on the sidewalk outside. The Muthaiga Country Club is as crisply Victorian as ever; and your typical British bachelor accountant fulfilling a two-year contract employs a houseboy who for ten shillings a day and two pounds of "staff meat," given him to take home to his wife for the week, will address the bwana as "Bwana." However, because the situation is complicated, the Britisher himself will say "Bwana" occasionally, when in need of a favor from a clerk or a porter.

For weeks I rode buses, partly on a camping safari, because I, too, had come to look at the animals. Having written about North American wildlife, I wanted to find out if there was something to add about these floral giraffes and priapic rhinos, the airborne extravaganza of kites, storks, and vultures—such a profusion of life that the sunbird family alone is a whole brilliant constellation, and hyenas needed to be invented just to dispose of the detritus of it—which couldn't be said about wildlife already familiar to me. From the time we read *Babar*, in a sense no wildlife is more familiar than Africa's, and the spectators in a game park before they do anything else are confirming that these creatures, part of the furniture of childhood, really do live as they've been pictured and described.

But apart from retailing a few late discoveries in animal behavior, there seemed to be nothing fresh to convey. To write about animals anywhere nowadays is to write of the end of the world; yet I don't invariably believe in the end of the world. One no longer travels to Africa to experience "where we came from"—a dark continent of savages, the pool of the past—but, rather, to swim in the pool of the future. If there aren't more of "them" than "us," there soon will be. One has a humming sense in Africa of the world born anew. Four hundred million people, 45 percent of them under the age of fifteen: not the earth's densest population, but the fastest growing. Forty countries ten or twenty years old, seemingly intent upon recapitulating two centuries' worth of Latin American coups and counter-coups within a couple of decades. So much is going on that the life of a new visionary on the order of David Livingstone would be swallowed up all over again in exploring it.

What would absorb Livingstone this time around would be not the geography of Africa but the people, not the specter of slavery but hunger. One either believes that life is precious or not; and it isn't a decision so much as a discovery that one makes about oneself. Precious and wretched, perhaps—but the operative word is *precious*; and if the response is going to be yes, then the urgency of this continent strikes home. Out on the road, seeing from the bouncing bus a woman pounding cassava roots with pestle and mortar, hoeing yams in her shamba with a baby strapped to her hip and her older kids shooing the goats off, it seems as though time might take care of everything. But my bus broke down in Isiolo, a hot, famine-struck town on the edge of the northern desert scrubland that takes up two-thirds of Kenya, and I was so importuned by beggars of every description, beggars so desperate—gray, listless children, crawling men supporting themselves on sticks, women who'd carried a fifty-pound sack of charcoal six or eight miles on their heads for the equivalent of twenty cents—that I had nowhere to turn. These people were starving.

The adventure of African travel is no longer provided by lions and charging buffalo ("buff," Hemingway called them). Instead, it's the sudden roadblocks, the whimsy of new regulations at the border crossings—a police force and army created almost overnight. At a dinner party one can spend hours with several old Africa hands hearing nothing but their arrest stories. Six weeks in a minibus trying to get across the Central African Empire. A rifle butt through the windshield in Uganda—sitting there with a lapful of broken glass has been enough to unstring a good many Africa enthusiasts. Even in Kenya it is becoming commonplace for a European whose property has excited the avarice of a government official to be ordered to quit the country within twenty-four hours. Traditionally, Africa has attracted Europeans with something missing in them, some bit of the backbone gone, and its sternness together with its abundance stiffened and also soothed them. But the sternness is becoming a problem now. Only the other kind of expatriate—the alley cat—thrives.

In 1967 Kenya, Uganda, and Tanzania, emerging from the first convulsions of independence (two attempted coups in 1964, which the British had to come in and help suppress), formed the East African Community. Currency, mail service, telecommunications, taxing, and transport authority were to be shared. The postal service and East African Airways have worked out well, but the rest of the Community's cooperative ventures are languishing. Because of its success at drawing tourists and foreign investment, Kenya's money has twice the value of Tanzania's in under-the-counter foreign exchange; and, peevishly, Tanzania has been seizing Kenya-licensed vehicles that cross the border. As early as 1972 Idi Amin found cause to bomb the Tanzanian villages fronting Uganda, and lately has laid claim to a huge slice of Kenya territory, which (if combined with the Kenyan land that Somalia, to the northeast, claims) would reduce the country to the size of a peanut.

Amin is ridiculed in the Nairobi newspapers and generally described in Kenya as a primitive. President Julius Nyerere of Tanzania bitterly characterizes him as "Vorster's dream"—the sort of black bogeyman whom South Africa's prime minister can point to to justify continued white rule. Nyerere is a sober idealist who dresses in a severe-looking tunic and, as president, took out a loan from the bank to build a house for himself, eschewing the colonial grandeur of State House in Dar es Salaam. He has none of the raffishness that Amin and Jomo Kenyatta, of Kenya, share, nor the bloody-mindedness that Amin flourishes and Kenyatta sometimes hints at circumspectly (usually in Swahili).

Kenyatta is no Amin, however. He is more of a poor man's Haile Selassie, an Independence hero who in his eighties has gone venal and sour, and there is the possibility of succession problems when he dies that will compare with Ethiopia's difficulties once Selassie was eclipsed. So much corruption, centered, to begin with, on Kenyatta's own "royal family"—$180 million in charcoal exported illegally to the Middle East in the past two years, and $60 million in ivory to the Far East—must have an issue eventually. The slogan of the country, *Harambee* ("Let's all pull together," an old, rope-operated river ferryboat cry), has worked out to mean every man for himself, with unemployment in Nairobi, a city of six hundred fifty thousand, at 40 percent, the parks draped with sleeping sad sacks, and private guards posted with club in hand along every downtown street. A white man who barhops, if he doesn't get mugged, encounters a series of frantic con men, needy "students," each with a brother at Columbia University in the United States.

The other slogan in Kenya is "Africanization," which is to say that a man of the black elite, instead of an Asian or *mzungu* (white), should drive around in a Mercedes-Benz.

Accompanying black capitalism are the "parking boys," ten-year-old walking parking meters who scrape by one day away from hunger and sleep in small packs in the bushes—but also some of the virtues of capitalism elsewhere: not a free parliament, but relatively (for Africa) free speech out on the street, and a fairly lively press. The best newspaper is owned by the Aga Khan, in fact. The inner circle of the government cannot be attacked, but it's fun to see the newsmen go to work on, say, the foreign minister from Addis Ababa, on Nairobi's version of *Meet the Press*. Although at least three important dissenting figures have been assassinated in Kenya, and Kenyatta maintains a paramilitary force called by the sinister euphemism General Service Unit ("God Sent Us"), there are far fewer political prisoners in Kenya than in Uganda or Tanzania, and his regular army is only a modest one compared with the Soviet-supplied Ugandan and Somali battalions that sandwich him in. With his ceremonial white fly whisk, the evocative shield and crossed spears on his flag, and his frank, shrewd, but vaguely disreputable air, "the Old Man," as he is called, isn't without appeal.

All that Nyerere may have in common with Kenyatta is that Tanzania too is a "civilized" African country governed by some of the laws of logic that we Westerners recognize. Nyerere is closest ideologically to his Frelimo (Front for the Liberation of Mozambique) neighbors, and closest personally to Kenneth Kaunda, Zambia's president, accepting the idea that Kaunda leans West, just as he often leans East. He is a favorite charity of the Swedes, the Chinese Communists, the Dutch, the Canadians, and both West and East Germany, and the $38 million he got from the United States in 1975 was the highest dollar aid figure in all of black Africa. "Good value," they say at the American embassy in Dar es Salaam, because the money is spent on what it has been appropriated for, and Nyerere himself is earnest, consistent, and incorruptible, and his nonalignment appears to be genuine. He broke relations with Britain (since reinstated) over the question of Rhodesia's successful secession, sacrificing £10 million worth of aid to do so, but was the first head of state in Africa to denounce the Arab oil bloc for raising prices for the underdeveloped world at the same rate as for Europe and the United States. China built the *Uhuru* railroad to Zambia for him, but only after the World Bank and various other Western institutions had turned him down. He has gotten most of the Chinese out of the country by now, speaks angrily of the Soviets' refusal to assist, as the United States did, when drought brought famine to Tanzania in 1974, and when visiting a politics class at the University of Dar es Salaam, he will make the point that Marx wrote about the revolution of the proletariat but that Tanzania, with a populace 95 percent rural, effectively has no proletariat.

Still, the newspapers read like North Korea's, and the Foreign and Interior ministries are virulently anticapitalist. (The Treasury, Trade, and Agriculture bureaucracies appear rather pro-West, according to foreigners who deal with them.) Chinese toothpaste, shoes, and canned food fill the stores, in payment for that railroad, and although tourists from the decadent West are let into the country for purposes of foreign exchange, if they stray from the regular circuit of game parks like Ngorongoro and Serengeti and happen to run into a local zealot—a "ten-cell leader," as the lowest-rung TANU party functionaries are called—they may meet with some awful unpleasantnesses.

The Chinese model of rural communes has been useful to

Nyerere in fashioning his Ujamaa communities throughout the countryside. There are seventy-five hundred of these, each with a thousand people or more concertedly tilling the soil. Access is forbidden to foreigners, and with his haste in the past few years to transfer the bulk of the farming populace have come some accounts of rough stuff, former hamlets burned. Nyerere is also moving his capital from the pretty port of Dar es Salaam, with its half-million souls, to a barren town called Dodoma in the middle of the country, on the same quite dubious principle that evoked Brasilia in Brazil. He is nation-building, just as the Chinese had to, only more so. But what is interesting is how his conception of what he is after differs from Chinese Communism. First, he includes religious freedom in his plans—like him, a third of his countrymen are Christian, about a third Muslim, and a third animist—and he doesn't object to missionaries. Second, the sometime Chinese emphasis upon constant confrontation and revolution has been laid aside. Nyerere begins by assuming that everybody "is either a peasant or a worker," so there is no need to root out and obliterate a nebulous exploiter class; independence from Britain, he says, took care of that. Third, people can leave or return to Tanzania comparatively easily, if they wish. *Ujamaa* means "familyhood," and the purpose is to build upon the ancient African kinship customs, with handicapped citizens or the unemployed from the city put back into the care of their hometowns. But the system is intended to be so pervasive that even admission into the university is by permission of the local office of TANU.

It's said by disillusioned observers that the students are taught by a mixture of revisionist leftists from England and revisionist rightists from Czechoslovakia, and not very well. Too often the conspiracy theory of economics is applied to

explain Tanzania's poverty, rather than the circumstance
that she lets India manufacture rope from her sisal (one-
third of the year's crop needlessly burned on the Dar es Salaam docks soon after my visit), and that China makes tex-
tiles from her cotton, and England coffee from her red
beans. The minimum wage is above Kenya's, though, and
Nyerere has contrived to reduce the spread between the
highest- and lowest-paid government employees from seventy to one at the time of Independence to nine to one.

Nyerere is by all accounts a humane man, as in his treatment of lepers and criminals—there is no death penalty except on the island of Zanzibar, which exercises self-rule—
as well as in his concern for wild things. In Kenya, wildlife
translates mostly into tourism and cash, and is managed abruptly as such. In Tanzania, although the animals must finally pay for themselves in foreign exchange or find their
land wrested away from them, much is made of the fact
that the great game herds are a centerpiece of the nation's
heritage and should be preserved, and that tourism in the
future will be regional, as Africans see for themselves what
the continent holds.

But because Tanganyika—as mainland Tanzania used to be
called—was home to a hundred and twenty-two different
tribes, running counter to this policy of cultural conserva-
tion is the government's effort to wipe out tribal affiliations,
keeping all mention of tribal loyalties, except deprecating
references, out of the papers, for instance, and discourag-
ing foreign anthropologists who want to come in. *Ujamaa*
is to be substituted for the blood and language kinship of
the tribes. Nyerere himself came from a backwater group
that does not furnish him with a power base, unlike Kenyatta, whose mighty Kikuyu in Kenya have been his primary source of support all along. Thus in Kenya a man's

tribal origins are still spoken of, and Kikuyu is the third language of the country, after Swahili and English. Swahili, that old slaver's tongue—pidgin Bantu, pidgin Arabic—ironically has been the language of *Uhuru* ("freedom") in East Africa, and particularly in Tanzania, where the use of English, as well as the tribal dialects, is being phased out in school.

Nyerere is a moderate man who, unfortunately, has not institutionalized his own moderation. Nor has he picked vice-presidents of the same stripe. One of the two, Rashidi Kawawa, may have a cruel streak. He helped run a British detention camp for Kikuyu during the Mau Mau war, and chose to announce, then enforce, the nationalization of the whites' coffee farms under Mount Kilimanjaro right at the annual festive banquet of the growers, after the toasts to him and his government were done. The other individual, Sheikh Aboud Jumbe, is from Zanzibar, which is an ominous preparation for public office. There, clove smuggling is punishable by death; wearing a skirt that shows the knee, by four strokes of the cane; failing to raise a given quota of food, by six months in jail. No defense counsel is permitted in court, and executions are usually informal. In 1964 something like three thousand Arabs were massacred in the maze of Stone Town, after eight hundred years of Arab tyranny over the blacks.

A tourist in Zanzibar is treated with such velvety courtesy that I found it moderately terrifying. The police have the murderous look I remember from Salazar's Portugal, and everywhere one encounters that secret, basilisk, cat-that-swallowed-the-canary smile of people who have profited from a massacre, or else from the centuries of slaving before. Stepping off the plane, you are handed a malaria pill because the government has reversed its policy of a few years ago when it stopped an anti-malaria campaign on the grounds that only white people get malaria anyway, and white people ought to.

Zanzibar keeps $60 million stashed in a London bank, while mainland Tanzania limps along on infusions of Swedish kronor. Zanzibar boasted the first color television and the first Ferris wheel in black Africa, because of its near monopoly of the world's cloves, and has belts of Stalinallee architecture, courtesy of the East Germans. The Sultan's white palace has become a People's Palace, with a People's Garden outside, and lines of Swahili women garbed in Muslim black wait at the entrance to the V. I. Lenin Hospital to be treated by the Chinese staff. Because island republics such as the Seychelles are gaining nationhood close by, some Zanzibaris suspect that they may have made a mistake, rushing to link up with Tanganyika in 1964.

Only in Zanzibar did I feel I was in a "dictatorship"—to use the term that was being bandied about by our U.N. ambassador, Mr. Moynihan, at the time. I roamed through Tanzania by bus, and in the long, bouncing nights, sitting beside Chaggas, Sukumas, Masai (their spears in the baggage rack on top, unless two buses got in a race, whereupon the men would take back their spears, stick them through the windows, and rap the beast, urging it on), I found the mainland a freewheeling place. Certainly it is no "dictatorship" as Hitler and Franco and Stalin defined the term, nothing like traveling in Spain fifteen years ago. And Tanzania impressed me as a more relaxed, better-knit country than Kenya also, partly because there isn't the brutal contrast of wealth to poverty among the Africans themselves, and partly because there are fewer Europeans around, so that the Tanzanians aren't always looking over one shoulder at a diehard colonial smothering a smirk, a tourist subduing his impatience at the difference in how things operate here in Africa from the way they are at home.

If the caution and humanity that in general seem to come naturally to Nyerere—which has been shown again in his treatment of the Asian minority—can only be institutionalized, his country may wind up as the kind of showpiece the Scandinavian countries hope for. The population is expanding painlessly so far (2.7 percent, versus Kenya's 3.5 percent increase a year); and if Tanzania has less prime acreage than Kenya, more of its land can be marginally farmed. In some ways Kenya is a peppier country, however —not such a solemn test tube. The climate, the natural beauty, the wild animals, the luxury facilities, the general permissiveness, and the business "infrastructure" combine to bring in $75 million in tourism a year, to add to the foreign exchange earned by coffee and tea. Besides, there's a whiff of old-fashioned freedom in Kenya, which, if Kenyatta's successors can introduce a spirit of reform and solicitude for more of the people, may make it the happier country to live in someday.

But Dar es Salaam was my favorite city, in a six-week tour. No twisty-streeted little city could be more dramatic to enter at night. And at sunrise, when the dhow-rigged, outrigger *ngalawas* sailed in, a crowd of fish peddlers on bicycles collected for the auction of fish held on the beach. With all of the people who were lounging about, they stood as thick as if they were embarking upon a pilgrimage —black people with Arabian faces and brimless cloth hats. That funny language, Swahili ("automobile" is *motocaa*, "gonorrhea" is *kissinono*), rang out from the Indian auctioneer over each pail of fish that was dumped on the sand. Then the long hammerhead sharks, swordfish, and kingfish were sold individually. The official government-office band paraded by to rouse the spirits of people working inside. People bought coconuts, punched a hole in and drank, bought bananas, chewed *khat*. A little motorized ferry chuffed across the mouth of the harbor. The *Asia-Afrika*, a freighter from Canton, slid past our eyes. And wandering about, I was struck by how fascinating life is going to continue to be, how provincial we were, the Chinese, the Africans, and me. The world is ending for the elephants whose domed skulls I had seen alongside the Galana River in Kenya, but not for human beings.

Of course, America, even where she is unpopular, remains a magnetic image to new nations like these for her many innovations. Right now, it's our music, movies, good food, and clothes that seem to be the drawing card—experiments, for the most part, of fifty or sixty years ago. But our deeper experiments, both old and new, will take their turn.

1976

THE
FRAGILE
WRITER

Suddenly three are a number of first-rate women writers around—so many that one doesn't envy them the competition, if they are drawing anger and insight from the same well. It's an illustration again of how fragile a matter artistic fecundity is. Some sort of sea change occurs in the climate of opinion—an idea's time comes due—and almost immediately a group of writers materialize who had not made themselves available before.

The circumstances are different in this case, however. Writers, like other artists, have generally originated in the middle class since anybody started noticing origins at all; and so in America when a particular ethnic minority has stopped being either cops or robbers, commonly and quite abruptly its children have begun to publish novels, as in the post–World War II surge of Jewish, Irish, black, and Italian-American writing. But women—constituting half the country—had been going to college and enjoying the advantages of a good Protestant bank account, foreign travel, a polite neighborhood, a room of one's own, leisure in the evening, and whatnot for very much longer than they had chosen to exercise their prerogative to publish their opinions on any proportionate scale. They had been editors, for instance, but, from some arcane failure of nerve, had not stepped forward in numbers to speak for themselves until freed only recently by one of those fascinating tippings of the scales in the process that produces art.

I emphasize the fragility because it relates to the larger question of how people write. Anybody who occasionally visits writers at home will remember being astonished to discover that the well-known nature poet who eulogizes his backyard raccoons doesn't really know where the coons' den tree is, doesn't know a skink from an eft, in point of fact, or a warbler from a sapsucker, has never set foot in a canoe, and is afraid of mountain heights. The female novelist who writes explicitly of sex turns out to be a timid lover. The Civil War buff who throws himself so enthusiastically into descriptions of hard soldiering will confess that as a young man he concealed himself in graduate school in order to escape the draft. The memoirist who charmingly, forgivingly chronicles the crotchets of other writers seems less wise and generous in person, obsessed instead with literary politics.

Go to Yankee Stadium with the sportswriter whose books are said to have bejeweled the game of baseball. He is so carping, uncomfortable, and bored that he's no fun—watches with less absorption than the beer-belly sitting in the next box. Of course the problem is actually that he cares too much. The shuffle of reality pains him because it muddles the issues and is so slow, wasting the months as he waits for a certain telling detail that may help him to elucidate what the game is all about. To go back to a setting he has already written about is just as painful for an author, because, for one thing, he is probably afraid somebody there is going to want to punch him in the mouth. And he remembers, too late, an anecdote he never thought to include in his book, or sees an irresistible tableau that got away from him the first time around. Worse still (though contrariwise), he must fight off the suspicion that he is nothing but a hoaxer, that he inflated what was essentially a humdrum bunch of ordinary people into a whole hocus-pocus entirely his own.

Again and again, if you know a few writers, you run into the contrast between the imaginary worlds that they have fabricated and their real bumbling about in a territory which in real life they have not made theirs at all. Nonetheless, these infirmities don't greatly count. It's from his passion, not his experience, that a writer primarily writes. His passion is what is fragile, too; he realizes that by and by it's going to run out. Between books, or in the dreadful slump that sometimes afflicts him when he is two-thirds through a book, you will encounter him stretched out, practically in traction, with various vertebral twinges and aches, on his couch. Passing by an open door, you glimpse the famous, fierce, heterosexual woman novelist sitting weeping on the matronly lap of a surrogate mum. The notion persists that writing is accomplished from the ragged edge of the nerve ends—that one pours all one's desperation into it—but most good writing is by nature glandular, and happy when it's going well.

We hear also, though to the contrary, that innocence, the child's unspoiled eye, is the foundation of art. It would be as unfortunate if Gore Vidal were loaded down with such an appurtenance as if Maurice Sendak were not. Hand in glove, ambition goes along with the innocence, at any rate —a name-making kind of ambition that is less appetizing than the pecuniary variety. Like a roomful of senators, a clutch of writers at a cocktail party maneuver past each other with gingerly nods; and one of the first lessons that a youngster entering the craft should learn is that if he intends to disagree with anybody, he might just as well challenge the honcho publicly and not stint on the strong words, because a private letter of demurral will provoke the same intransigent grudge. Needless to say, the new literary alliances of former underdogs have proven no less brutal than the old black-hat league of WASPs who were resented for having run the show before. The savaging that was bestowed on Ezra Pound in 1972, while Pound swayed on the brink of the grave, by Irving Howe and several other Jewish literary lights, notwithstanding Pound's thirteen years of incarceration for sins of the mind, is an ugly example.

Still—and this might sound antediluvian—the quality that used to be spoken of as personal "character" has a substantial influence in the practice of writing. It operates least where there is a suggestion of genius involved, but even then, in a case such as Nabokov's (not to mention Pound's), some mortal crimp in the man's soul, some minginess of spirit has foreshortened his achievement when set against the power of his gifts. With the average writer, the holes one notices in him from knowing him are usually duplicated in his work. An incapacity for love, an inability to come to terms with the opposite sex, an overfastidious distaste for children, a fear of getting to know people, a tin ear for suffering, an autodidact's smugness or an Ivy League snobbery, the vice of perennial experimentation, a weakness for enlisting himself in every flibberty new cause or vogue —the list of instances could go on.

And so the young writer sets out with a full curly head of talent and a tense tic for work, and with a vivid piece of subject matter as green and crisp as romaine lettuce in his hands. He storms the barricades he saw in front of him, but beyond them perhaps he only flounders into the same miserable mishmash inside himself that turned him toward the solitary pursuit of writing to start with. Gradually he begins to play the ham a bit instead of working quite as honestly, "retiring," as it is said of writers, "to public life." The reed that whistled dauntlessly for him at first is broken.

1976

GREAT
ADVENTURES

Travel, travel—never so much of it, as people try to catch the peak of the autumn in New England, then tuck a vacation into the dead of winter, or experience a double spring by flying south in March. Yet travel books remain the weak sisters of literature, feeble both in the bookstores and in most critics' esteem. Unquestionably, they do lack thickness of a sort that only the characters of a good novel or play provide. We know our author survived in the end, so there is little "suspense," and meanwhile he describes his encounters with everybody just in passing, before moving on. Far from spinning out his family history for us, or a tale of the loves of his life, he is probably turning deliberately away from family and love.

Many of the best travel writers are odd ducks. They are likely to twist around when you least expect it and undergo a sex-change operation (Jan Morris), or to be accused of a generalized kinky prevarication (T. E. Lawrence) in the light of later research. Several superlative travelers, such as H. M. Stanley, gathered about them a reputation for extraordinary brutality in their day. Some preferred native to Caucasian women, or liked little boys. As is true of so many nature writers, a lot of them give off a whiff of the cold fish, at least, and because traveling became commonplace only recently, its arduousness as we remember it makes us distrust them, besides. Why didn't they stay home like everyone else? Marco Polo reports that on the eastern coast of India in the thirteenth century sailors were not permitted to testify at a trial or to be legal guarantors, "for they say that a man who goes to sea must be a man in despair."

Traveling was a compelling profession, however; and if we are such travelers now, why do so few of us know the journals of Peter Kalm, William Bartram, George Catlin, John James Audubon, Lewis and Clark, John W. Powell, John Muir, just to name some of the obvious candidates among the pathfinders of an earlier America who kept diaries and also seem to have been reasonably decent souls? Or, if we limit ourselves simply to the greatest of all explorers —Captain Cook, in his flat-bottomed coaling ships, and Marco Polo, by land—why aren't their accounts of supremely adventurous voyages read as routinely as literary masterpieces (which it is understatement to say that they are not)? Why isn't Captain Cook as familiarly known as Tom Jones?

James Cook, a laborer's son, was kaleidoscopic in his talents as a seaman and, in conduct, humane. For example, in 1777 he went out of his way to bring safely back to Tahiti a native of that island, Omai, whom he had transported to London for exhibit three years before. But Cook was both

terse and cluttered in his jottings, so that his editors have
become his collaborators.

Marco Polo's *Travels* is an as-told-to book, composed by
a cellmate of his—one Rustichello of Pisa, who by good
fortune happened to be a veteran writer of romances—during a year of confinement they shared as prisoners of war in
Genoa. All the same, *The Travels* lacks a narrative line,
proceeding instead like a museum tour. There are the har-
poonists of the Arabian Sea who first intoxicate a carnivo-
rous whale with pickled fish, then stand on his head as he
swims along and knock the spear down through his skull.
Condemned criminals in India, as a point of honor, will cut
off their own heads with a two-handled knife. Zanzibari elephants breed by means of a hollow the bull digs in the
ground, into which he lays the female, supine. The currency of the great Kublai Khan is manufactured from mul-
berry bark, Marco Polo says, but this conqueror of Peking
has ordered prairie grass to be planted in the courtyard of
his palace to remind him of the freedom of the open spaces
he has left behind. He tours with a pavilion of three enormous tents covered with lion skins and lined with ermine,
and whenever he takes up his cup to drink, ten thousand
barons and other guests fall to their knees. Fish-eating sheep;
herbs that, when eaten, make the hooves fall off a horse's
feet. Maidens who, as they walk, never advance one foot
more than a finger's breadth in front of the other, so as not
to impair their proof of virginity. Alongside the funeral
procession of Mongu Khan, twenty thousand human beings
were put to death to serve the dead king in the afterlife.

All these separate dioramas—though justification enough,
coming as they do from the greatest explorer who ever
mounted a horse, meeting swordsmen on horseback who, as

he says, had "made up their minds to conquer the whole world"—are linked solely by the adventurer's curiosity, nonetheless. It is our own wonder and delight that meld them into a book and not merely a document. Neither Marco Polo nor the khans who were his patrons, nor the commoners with whom he shared this passage of twenty years, linger in the mind: only the spectacle of the East itself.

Marco Polo's *Travels* was written in 1299. If we swing ahead two and a half centuries, we discover a much more personal travel writer and autobiographer in the vain, extravagant, exuberant personage Benvenuto Cellini, a genius goldsmith with a murderer's temper. Maybe because he worked at diminutive pieces of precious metal in an age of heroic stone sculpture, such as his friend Michelangelo did, Cellini's tantrums were proportionately eruptive. He was always shifting from Rome to Florence to put himself under the protection of the Medici dukes in order to escape the bailiffs of the Pope; then back to Rome because of a crime of passion or "treason" in Florence. In six months he would go north again, to Siena, or straight on to Paris and the court and protection of Francis I. So often his pleasure in traveling is that he has dodged a pack of assassins, eluded the *bargello*, or even the threat of the stake (when a French servant girl charged him with buggering her).

Cellini informs us that as a cannoneer he is a crack shot, defending—"saving"—the Castel Sant' Angelo for Pope Clement against the army of the Constable of Bourbon. Later he suffers a most wretched imprisonment in the identical castle, his teeth falling out from malnutrition, till he escapes by descending from a dizzy height on knotted bed sheets. Worse than a braggart, he is irrational, an exceedingly dangerous specimen: he commits neat little murders

—the knife slipped into the soft tissue just under the ear. When he loses a lawsuit he is likely to hamstring the plaintiff, and can kill a man with a stone to the temple, or will blast an obdurate tenant out of an apartment he wants for himself. As a hustling craftsman, he has worked several German assistants to death, he announces, but broken in health at one point, he retires to Ferrara and feasts upon peacocks. Later, distracted by these unending feuds, he commits an unforgivable lapse—his two-year-old son is smothered by a vicious nurse, after begging his father to rescue him from her care. Still, the descriptions Cellini gives of the incomparable beauty and intricacy of his creations are convincing, and, rogues that we are too, we stick with him—except for that horrible lapse—through accounts of vomiting popes, of dukes who order a merchant to "blow your chaps out till I smack them," apprentices kicked "in the fork of the legs," and of innumerable "light" but "clean" wenches.

Cellini's autobiography is at present a neglected classic, less read, it would seem, than in the time of Mark Twain, who made confident reference to it. But on occasion the selfishness of so many of Cellini's endeavors does pall, when set next to Marco Polo's readiness to explore the entire earth, or—a better example—Bernal Díaz del Castillo's inspired memoir, *The True History of the Conquest of New Spain*. This latter book, which recounts Hernando Cortez's march through Mexico fifty years after the event, was put down as a labor of love during almost the same years as Cellini was writing his story, both authors being old men by then. Cellini died in 1571, seven years after the end of his narrative, and Bernal Díaz a decade later than that, in his eighties.

"What I myself saw, and the fighting in which I took

part, with God's help I will describe quite plainly, as an honest eyewitness, without twisting the facts in any way. I am now an old man . . . and have lost both sight and hearing; and unfortunately I have gained no wealth to leave to my children and descendants, except this true story," Díaz begins.

Modest, intimidated by the prospect of writing for the illumination of learned men, he is a contrast to the vainglorious Cellini. (Appropriately, there is an entry in the dictionary for "Cellini's halo"—meaning the phenomenon *Heiligenschein.*) But Díaz was sustained by his shimmering memories: those Indian chiefs with tall plumes and feather clothing, eating rose-scented cakes for luncheon, who sometimes lodged in dwellings so burnished with lime that they appeared to have been constructed of silver. Like Cellini, Rabelais, and other contemporaries, Díaz was alive to the whole menagerie of smells of his era; and, like Marco Polo, was a man elated by the sight of a sweep of virgin grass, or an army mustering, even against himself. He tells us of a plain six miles deep and six miles across, crowded with warriors with turtle-shell shields and cotton armor, such as suited warfare with arrows, opposing the four hundred Spaniards. The arrows flew like locusts and the locusts like arrows, in disastrous confusion. Captain-General Cortez would have already sent to the *cacique* the best that he had in the way of a whimsical gift. Once, to the Tlascalans, he tendered a long-piled, red Flemish hat, but the present did not succeed as a peace offering, and was instead proffered by them to their idols after the battle, together with the four iron shoes of a horse they had killed. Cortez had augmented his tiny force as best he could with sailors from his ships—he had destroyed the ships—and with six individuals belonging to a rival expedition, whom he had kidnapped.

For the longest interval, the white men and their horses were regarded as godlings by the Indians, and as one and the same. The horsemen, charging at a trot, held their lances high, aiming for the face, never stopping to spear an adversary through the body, lest the lance be wrenched away. Both their wounds and the horses' injuries they dressed with fat from enemy corpses, and very soon began to traffic in Indian girls as well as to court them. Díaz was given a chieftain's daughter by Montezuma himself.

Montezuma's capital rode like a second Venice on the surrounding waters when three of Cortez's soldiers glimpsed it from the summit of Sierra de Ahualulco. They all entered peacefully that first time, discovering a marketplace as large as Rome's or Constantinople's, and the famous pyramids with temples on top, and cannibal priests with blood-grisly hair. For safety's sake, they took captive the vacillating emperor, with his gold-soled shoes, along with many "kinglets," who were attached by the neck to a single stout chain. But much perilous fighting followed on the causeways and drawbridges of the city—a retreat with losses of nine hundred out of a force grown to thirteen thousand Spaniards. The Indians whistled, blew trumpets and conch shells, and pounded kettle drums as they attacked by the tens of thousands, and many Spaniards drowned because of the loads of gold they had strapped to their shoulders.

After further campaigns, intrigues, and stratagems, and further battle wounds sustained by the author, Cortez's expedition prevailed, it goes without saying. And the affectionate, shrewdly checkered portrait of the conqueror, as well as that of brave, fearful Díaz himself, lifts *The True History* to a brilliance and permanence on a par with the feats of arms that are described. In fact, no travel book about what we call Latin America can stand beside Díaz's

chronicle—unless we jump ahead again four centuries to
Claude Lévi-Strauss's masterpiece of intellect, observation,
and melancholy, *Tristes Tropiques*, which gains its power
from an inner momentum, as most modern books do.
We've seen too many events, too many conquests. A Ren-
aissance bloody-mindedness working excitedly over the
bloody embroilments of our own day would seem gro-
tesquely ill-tuned.

We do still have travel books—and not just the lively recent variety by young British-oriented writers like Bruce
Chatwin and Paul Theroux. John Steinbeck and Saul Bel-
low, on the homestretch to their respective Nobel prizes,
produced rather winsome, nice-tempered volumes which,
although uninteresting compared with their earlier work,
rounded off their careers winningly. But people remain un-
convinced that anything momentous is left to be discovered
by traveling. Travel is for diversion, they think, and not for
spelunking.

1978

WOMEN
AND
MEN

One reason the effects wrought by the Women's Movement remain clouded in uncertainty is that its goals have been divided between matters of simple justice and matters of androgyny. The simple part is that any fair-minded person who walks into a bank and sees that all the tellers are women and all the officers are men is going to cast a vote for women's rights. This might not have been the case a dozen years ago—nor is it now in backwoods America—any more than other principles of social justice that we regard as elementary have always been considered so. But powerful inertial forces opposing change in the United States have a way of abruptly caving in; and nowadays most people who learn that women are discriminated against in questions of jobs, salary, access to education, or property rights are going to react the same. That battle, however painful, has been uncomplicated and, except for what amounts to a mopping-up operation, seems to have been won.

What is utterly unknown, unwon, is the extent of the changes in sexuality itself that are under way. Some women activists wanted men to cease to exist. Others wanted women to become like men. Others wanted women to become like men and men to become like women, in the old sense—while still others wanted everybody to become the same, somewhere in between.

The mainstream of the Movement took an attitude on the subject too ambiguous to put into words. It both did and didn't wish for punitive as well as substantive change. It both did and didn't advocate equality between the sexes in complex, potentially anguished areas like child custody and alimony law and military service. It both did and didn't look forward comfortably to a bisexual world.

Usually, one need only see one's mother, if she is over sixty, to recognize that an immense, recent inequity existed between what the two sexes could do in the span of their lives. And yet a lot of confusion arose because of the comparison the Movement drew between this struggle and the civil rights movement of ten or fifteen years before. Linking them was an effective tactic for adding momentum, righteousness, and rage to the new cause, and plenty of people actually came to believe that middle-class white women in suburban America were a trod-upon underclass that had suffered injuries equatable to the mean and savage constrictions that had been imposed upon American blacks. To say that such a notion is absurd is not to belittle the wrong done to that row of underpaid bank tellers, who could work for twenty years with never a chance to advance themselves. But the result has been that any solution sounded so easy. If women were essentially identical with men, another institutionalized outrage could be set right, another long-suffering "minority" could be integrated into the vast, egalitarian mega-class through what by now has become quite standard methods of corrective laws and pressure politics. If women and men could be compared with rival ethnic constituencies, the imbalance between them could be construed as having originated only through prejudice, not biological imperatives. If men and women have no more need for each other *as* men and women than black people have for Caucasians as Caucasians—if they could now merely blend together—then legal remedies would be able to deal with the difficulties quite handily.

This is not to suggest our customs are not due for a profound overhaul. Apart from the issue of what is right, there are enough new imperatives arising from technology to have seen to that. But it will be an overhaul reaching to the wellsprings of how we express our love and lead our lives and how children are raised. Two by two, we've gone into Noah's Ark—or wherever we wanted to go—and to have gone always in twos implies some innate difference between the parties who have joined hands. Otherwise it could have been done as well in ones or threes or fours.

Surely, also, not just considerations of unit efficiency created this arrangement for raising a family. There must have been a feeling that life was thinner when lived either homosexually or in harem style—that a partner picked from Column A went best with one from Column B, and that the pairing probably thereafter should be adhered to. Where feminism has argued that Columns B and A should be equal by custom and before the law, it is not at all the same as saying there aren't and never should have been two columns. In primitive cultures, polygyny or polyandry did sometimes ensure that the most vigorous members of a tribe had the most mates and descendants. But "serial polygamy" in the form of divorce, as we now have it, does not necessarily do that, because modern-day divorce, even though accepted as a social alternative, is seldom such a sign of vigor, balance, and initiative as in those cultures the acquisition of several wives or husbands used to be.

My own reaction has been to agree, slowly, sometimes too begrudgingly, with most of the proposals for social equity the Movement made. But always I was astonished at how easy the proponents have thought the whole thing was going to be, once the Neanderthals arrayed against them had been overcome. It was as if two races from different continents that had been adventitiously brought into bitter conflict were to exchange declarations of understanding in order to have peace.

In lovemaking, "These are my nipples, but there are *your* nipples," said the representative from Atlantis, working diligently as a political act to awaken them to the same level of sensitivity as hers. "This your penis," she continued. "But *this* penis, which is called a clitoris, is *my* penis." And, indeed, although a penis corresponds not to the clitoris but to the vagina or uterus in its central importance to a man, for the moment it seemed she was right. That her hips were large was an embarrassment, even an affront, to her.

Not long ago (to take a literary example), Ernest Hemingway and other writers of the hairy-chested school were receiving such a chivvying for their roosterly preoccupations that an alarmist might have wondered whether some precious part of our admiration for bigger figures—like Homer's Achilles and Shakespeare's Henry V, and real-life heroes, such as Garibaldi—might also go by the boards. But women have generally taken such men to their hearts, just as other men do. Such a whole-hog, sustained assault against old-fashioned masculinity was never in the cards. Instead, the scope to emulate traditional heroes is being lost; and this, more than any sectarian animosity, will be what changes literature—people may not remember what Homer was talking about.

A crowded, tight, computerized world with regimentation that begins with a prenatal forecast of gender and extends to the grave must be more "feminine" in its field of action, regardless of the success or failure of any concerted effort to dismantle "masculinity," as it has been known. Masculinity must have more range, more space to operate in, because of the implication it carries that force may be used. Fistfights, pig slaughtering, river-swimming, home-brewed liquor, a hunting rifle in the closet, a mufflerless jalopy smoking from the tail pipe, or a no-prisoners-are-taken policy in a corporate boardroom set-to: these are "male." On the other hand, it would be reasonable to assume that a woman who is a sales manager in a cutthroat business and jogs four miles every evening for relaxation can read *The Iliad* as vividly as anybody who happens to possess male genitalia.

There will be people more taken with the sensibility of Jane Austen, and people who prefer Herman Melville, without reference to their own gender, sex as such having come to matter much less. We will have statistical improvements in every Olympic sport, ever-superior performances on the cello and at figure skating, while fame, as lately, continues to be quick, neuter, and bankable, emphasizing not only self-promotion, but a homogenized celebrity, so that new faces can be substituted easily. It is already impossible to paddle a canoe anywhere that hasn't got a zip code, and our admirable competitions in the marathon are not run in wild, open country, where they might convey the authority of an

151

ancient marathon, but as though under glass, through the middle of Boston and New York City, as glorified folk festivals.

It's admirable that so many people can run twenty-six miles, now when they no longer need to, and that upwards of two million New Yorkers are willing to leave their telephones long enough to watch them. And of course the argument that liberty has diminished with all this shrinking of operational territory and (as it seems to me) options of temperament—with the decline in regional distinctions, individual responsibility, and sexual definition, and the swing toward an egalitarianism of the lowest common denominator, by which, for example, a prospective President must run for office for many years full time—can be stood on its head. There is evidence, on the contrary, of an unprecedented freedom. With so many "subcultures," the pleasure of variety is everywhere. More people may be living in different ways than was imaginable before. Even for a macho man, no doubt, another brand of liberty is in the offing whenever, blindly feeling around, he manages to locate it.

Plenty of women in their twenties and thirties do evince a rare exuberance; one meets older women who sharply envy them the era they have been born into. And if, accordingly, many men of twenty-eight or thirty-three tend to display a peculiar muteness, it is not that they have special cause for complaint but that they are "not themselves," in the apt phrase—which is exactly what the feminist revolution has demanded. Very young men, bearing expectations better rooted in the chameleon realm of androgyny, appear to be more cheerful. And middle-aged men, although perhaps caught in the familiar hodgepodge of mid-life misdoubts and ironies like middle-aged women, nevertheless may confess to having had the best of both worlds.

As young men, they were prepared to rule the roost like Chanticleer, but now they watch the parade of change with quite a sympathetic interest, such as older men feel for younger women anyway, which often outweighs the sort of fatherly favoritism that they otherwise might direct toward younger men.

The women most vocal in Women's Lib haven't wished to concede the intricate interdependence that has existed between women and men, because to acknowledge such a complication would be to grant that unpredictable and agonizing problems might arise. Still, as a codicil to their prognostications, they have added the encouragement that men also are going to be liberated from unnecessary or discomforting constraints. One can see, in fact, that women, being franker and more approachable, have made the ritual of courtship a good deal easier, softening the old charade men had to go through in trying to win over a leery but conniving adversary with small lies and legerdemain. And when they work, it is a considerable convenience to the former "breadwinner." Even in high-strung professions like the law or public relations, women are by no means unanimous in advocating that men be unmanned and women masculinized until everybody starts from a hermaphrodite position, there to allow the personality to bend as it will. If young women are happier, so much the better for everybody; and on the tender question of who raises the children, possibly television raises them now anyway.

Technology is more leveling than feminism, as is the density in which we live, and our fat standard of living, combined with its recent shrinkage. (That is, we are left with less room to stretch out in a show of either masculine or feminine fervor—only the fat.) Not all the married women muscling into the commercial arena to earn a living really want to; and no military provision remains for young men to test themselves without the risk of a push-button war. Nor can young men afford the gasoline to drive from Atlanta to Seattle and back, the way they used to do as a substitute for going to war. After one gets through being glad that boys no longer have to prove that they are brave and strong, one begins to wonder whether an offbeat soul who wanted to could find a rip in the protective padding of bureaucratic regulation that surrounds us in order to accomplish such a coup.

We have to trust that people won't obliterate themselves in their inventions. Genetically, we are nearly identical to mankind fifty thousand years ago; and some of us delight in the continuity represented by this, while others may be appalled. But we count on each other—that the other fellow won't cross the highway divider in his car and knock us dead, won't molest our children on the way to school, won't accuse us of committing a crime we didn't do. In political, civil, and money matters we depend on one another, just as in the arts there could be no drama, music, painting, poetry if there were no community of response. Clasping a lover, feeling a heartbeat, one doesn't immediately know whose blood it is—and there is a triumph in this. Maybe eventually, in the same way, people won't care what biological equipment a lover has. And yet the pleasure of love-making derives from two people repeatedly trying to position themselves as opportunely as they can for insemination to occur. They can murmur nothings in the meantime, or vary the approach by trying to climb headfirst inside each other for a prenatal interlude. But the final sensation is basically just such as will best serve to help us replicate ourselves.

The differences between the sexes used to be exaggerated

to create a worse imbalance in rights and duties, but this was not only so that men could amass more power of the purse and of the sweets of life; it was also because a woman needed to mother six or eight children if two or three of them were to reach adulthood. In 1800 American women bore an average of seven children apiece, in the process of settling the continent. From their very bellies they produced a family; and one of the dislocations of feminism has been not to allow for the complexity of the War between the Sexes, as that half-humorous battle used to be called. Like the conflict between the generations, it had at its core real dissimilarities, as well as opportunism and bullying. Each sex belittled the other's pretensions and anatomical protuberances, and agreed to certain bitter tradeoffs, which, though not fairly balanced, appeared yet more inequitable when looked at from one side or the other—the husband's unofficial permission to stray from fidelity, versus the wife's to "take him to the cleaners" and keep the children in a divorce. But even in a man's world, women exercised substantial veto power. They helped determine who had children and who did not, who slept well and who endured insomnia, who was relatively contented and long-lived and who scarcely contrived to get his bags unpacked. "Behind every good man," the saying went, though recently there has been a commotion about how weak and shaky men are, as if this were a revelation, not the original discovery of "Nursing," that first bastion of the female professional.

Women, waiting out the sexual urgencies of men, have insisted upon some show of strength or nervous energy in a partner, as well as love and kindness, and all the lavish emblems of success and a commitment to the way of the world —but more fragile, nonconformist virtues, too, lest these be lost. The man as suitor buys flowers as a token of his earning power and in appreciation of the lady's finer tastes, yet in the tableau that they go through he must also smell the flowers appreciatively and admire them himself. He must moon with her by moonlight, as well as make big bucks under the bright light of the sun.

From their urge for permanence, women have generally avoided love affairs outside their own social class. The built-in passion for the female body that men are saddled with has created a constant dilemma for them: Did the gentleman want the lady in particular that he was with, or just an all-night squeeze? Was his love so abiding that it would transfer to the child that she might have by him? Did he "need" his ladylove enough, did he pay enough attention to her to stick by her through the task of feeding, as well as conceiving, babies? Was he conventional enough to make a go of things—yet, at the same time (and passion tested him for this), could he weather sleepless nights, did he have a sense of joy and fun, did he come back after a rebuff or when the woman whom he said he loved didn't look her best? And she, too—could she do without sleep? Was she clever or beautiful enough even in periods of discouragement to persuade another person to try to have more babies with her or at least continue to put food on the table for the earlier ones, instead of setting out to look for other ladies to make more babies with?

Though one knows women who enjoy playing with a man's body with the same utilitarian satisfaction that a man would feel in making free with theirs—women with grown children who cast a roving eye, women undergoing the trauma of divorce with the same frenetic sexual reaction that many men have felt, adventurous younger women who have set themselves a cutoff date of thirty or so, when they hope to turn "serious"—at least up until now, most women are far from being as casual about sex as a man. Nevertheless, besides the wish for steadiness, many have had a taste for what was reckless and randy in a man, looking especially for physical vigor or daring, or looked particularly to "trade up," with respect to social class. Many a woman has preferred the man who set his hat at a tilt and touched her leg without first asking if he could—except that the pain of that choice was that he might not go slow afterwards. For practical reasons, she has needed to choose one partner and try to hold him to fidelity, whereas, in theory—with his body tooled to father not just two or three children but hundreds—he could mate again and again. And so she has delayed expressing her preference, cultivating her good looks, waiting for him to choose her first, then prove his loyalty.

Some men have their heartstrings tied to their children and suffer an awful wrench if they lose them in a divorce. Still, they have that opposing imperative—to plant more offspring, not only among their contemporaries but in the next generation, and with ladies of the Left and Right, ladies who blow the trumpet and ladies who play the harp. This tension between the sexes enriches as well as afflicts us, having evolved by a primeval path. And though once in a while a Movement figure has warned the lesbian or radical wings against indulging in an open hatred of men—cautioning, for instance, that the occasional crime of rape should not be interpreted as a whole-cloth hatred of all women by all men—there has been too little recognition that the angry ebullience, the crowing and the snapping back and forth between the sexes, is not just connected with the issues of the moment but is an age-old torque.

No one is so fragile as a woman, but no one is as fragile

as a man. A lady, in sitting on my lap, becomes my child, but when she unbuttons her blouse, I become her child. A balance is struck, yet not a flattening balance of the kind that would make men and women the same. Her strengths make me feel strong, as do her weaknesses, and she says mine operate similarly. If this were not the case, our love-making would become only a business of rubbing two sticks together and our affections would level out to a primitive state. A revolution moving toward bisexuality under the umbrella of civil rights for women will be profound indeed, but because so much of sex is simulated anyway, no one can predict how drastically sex is likely to change.

In sex and love, contradictions abound. The responsive woman who moistens almost visibly when she perceives a comely professional man wearing the flush of conquest—put somebody in her path who *isn't* a comer, whose ribs she can feel, and she will sometimes bend above him, opening to his needs until she feels his ribs grow tallowy. If two men love her, they may hate each other or may become the best of friends. Although it's sexy if she is gentle, it can also be sexy if she's ungentle; and though most women don't want a kinky lover, a little stitching of kinkiness in him will prolong and spice their pleasure. The oldest riddle is that the same woman who draws men and glances wholesale, as though she had been brought into being expressly for procreation, is often mediocre as a mother. Yet that woman with the passion-peach complexion who might not wish to mother children—how deliciously she mothers men! The less in need they really are, the better. She turns apricot. We see the uneasy long legs, the breasts like brandy snifters (though modestly covered), the tumbling hair; and yet alongside these importunings, perhaps in the straight neck, sits an aloof boy.

It's no coincidence that boys could play Shakespeare's female roles rather convincingly, because part of what attracts a man to a woman is a swirl of emanations from her that resembles "boyishness"; and vice versa. The juice of sex is the consent of two adults to go to bed together, but counter to that, they both do look for secret semblances—plump Momma, and so on. Probably the biggest discovery of a young man's sexual awakening is that whatever he wants to do is not so far removed from what his girlfriend wants. So this could be called a species of androgyny, as is so much of the more complicated playacting, the chameleon coloration, of sex later on. It's an androgyny we are familiar with, however, an androgyny like that of Henry V himself, as Shakespeare imagined him in a play that is entirely predicated upon the fact that the hero king actually existed as a warrior, wooer, ruler, lover. Utterly masculine, Henry was androgynous because playful. But remove him as a sounding board, and you would have an art without echoes, history as archaeology—what was it *like* when there were men and women?

Sex draws us back into society from self-absorption. The ocean beach, the lights along the skyline, soon lose their romance if we have no company to enjoy them with. And our breadth of sympathy for other people is expanded if there is even a distant possibility that we might become sexual partners with them. A friend of mine, now married to a district attorney, had as her last lover a man under indictment for draft evasion. Another friend is married to a golf pro and dresses in the height of Miami sports fashion, but was first married to a professional woodsman and rattlesnake hunter. Men's hearts, too, have always gone out to the proverbial waitress and the proverbial duchess in quick succession, noticing their various vulnerabilities all the more because they are of the opposite sex. The $60,000-a-year executive, whose cough is unexpectedly deep-voiced in the morning, but whose soft excesses of flesh almost seem to "ask" for cancer because they are appendices without a function now, first had to struggle out of the posh suburbs, where her husband's salary had put her, in order to struggle back in.

Nor has the endless priapism of men much function lately; and the recent increased stress on sado-masochism—the agony attached to sexual fantasy—may be the result. Sex both as a tranquilizer and as the apple of contemporary existence may be nearly as necessary nowadays as the old sex of procreation was, though the tension it assuages is partly of its own making. Endless priapism, but no resolution. From a practical standpoint, it might seem absurd that men still wear two balls and women two breasts, as if they had need for them; yet—though it comes to nothing—people probably enjoy more bouts of sex than ever before. At least, the practice has spread more democratically through society, and is continued later in life, although big breasts as an ideal would seem to parody the actualities of the situation.

We struggle to complete ourselves—male with female, chatterbox with suppressed personality, blond-haired soul who hugs the exotic personage whose hair is black. And the extraordinary mating leap we make is possible only because there is a gap to leap. If acrimony alone were the upshot of the barriers that separate the sexes, their collapse would not be missed. But, under unisex, will we leap at all? And when the sex organs have been reduced to instruments of light pleasure, will the ecstasy of climax—losing even its present tenuous connection with childbearing—keep only its imitation of death at the end?

Anybody who remembers the persecution homosexuals suffered until recently will be in favor of some degree of androgyny. Yet nobody knows, and few people wish to think about, the significance of homosexuality in the new order of things. Is it a manifestation of neurosis, or not? Are rights to be accorded homosexuals that are appropriate to a religious-political minority, or to a "handicapped" minority? How will the limits of their normalcy be defined —up to and including marriage and the right to adopt children? The infant science of psychology is asked to decide whether an unabashedly homosexual grade-school teacher will influence the budding sexuality of his (her) students. Will the thinness—if it is a thinness—of homosexual life spread everywhere with bisexuality? And is androgyny or bisexuality any different from a dozen other forms of homogenization that are under way in the lives we live?

Perhaps, nevertheless, sexual intercourse will remain a deep, not light, pleasure, of profound significance, whatever the pretext for it may be. Perhaps, indeed, the Reagan and Moral Majority electoral landslide is not merely a sort of "Ghost Dance" of American cultural conservatism (as I tend to believe), but a genuine reversal of direction. Or on the contrary, androgyny may be an irresistible phenomenon, not to be opposed by "Ghost Dance" political movements or wistful traditionalists of a less hidebound stripe, such as me—a natural means of birth control, in other words, for a society gradually growing old.

Sex has always been "dehumanizing," as the saying goes —for Samson, and occasionally for everybody else. Yet part of why we emphasize it so perfervidly in an age when nature outdoors is dwindling is just that it *is* dehumanizing —animal, "natural." Better than baseball or jogging, it lifts us out of our envelopes of propriety. What a relief it would be in other corners of one's life to do exactly what one does in a romance—lean one's lovesick head against the lady's shoulder and ask indulgence and understanding. To tremble, sleepless from picturing somebody else, and then be able to lay one's face against that person's back and breast—this is luxury, just as is the "animal" rassling and thrashing.

But the flip side of our mating leap is the inconstancy that often characterizes friendship between the sexes. We will confess the scary cancer operation, the close brush with a nervous breakdown, while touching hands during that first all-night conversation. Splurging every dearest detail of a childhood spent on the Arkansas River, a Bronze Star won under zany circumstances on the Mekong River, we want the other person to know the very best and worst of us. Yet, a month later, in mutual exasperation, we claim we never want to see each other again. Although at any other time we are disgusted by other people's body by-products, we had tried to swallow each other's tongue. Neglecting our friends (an offense for which we will now probably try to make the lover pay), we had poured out our hearts—the young lawyer for Westinghouse who still harbors a faint, secret ambition to become Secretary of State, the young advertising copywriter who labors over her diary at night in hopes of blossoming like Virginia Woolf, now absolutely try to cut the rope. Teenagers like to say, "I'll never speak to you again," a more explicitly frightening threat in such a social stage of life as theirs.

Of course the criticism usually made of homosexual affairs is that *they* are too fragile or short-lived. But the passionate fragility of a homosexual love affair does not really correspond to the all-or-nothing commitment of two people who are preparing to raise children together. It is instead, in this respect, a make-believe, a dead end. Heterosexuals break off so sharply because they are looking for a partner in a twenty-year task. They must preserve an edge of total involvement for the love to come. Better a fresh start. Tear free suddenly and get away intact.

Life is surely still somewhat at risk, still full of opportunities to rely on oneself, with the fanning out that people do, in lives "laid back" or intense. The change toward serial or temporary marriages amounts to a new mode of isolation, spiritual more than physical, and the lady who began by listening to you as attentively as a geisha on your first evening together ends the affair by lighting up a cigarillo, as she gruffly tells you that you and she are through.

The right to a legal abortion is central to feminist demands, and, by its nature, cannot be guaranteed by applying the concept of "equal access." Plenty of women who recognize that the current rightward-moving pendulum in politics offers no serious threat to their recently won civic and professional mobility feel on accasion, though, an atavistic panic that above their rib cage they are forever hostage to what lies below; that only with the option of abortion can they be as free as a man. And their claim seems reasonable to me—a tragic but necessary trade-off that contemporary life requires. I'm offended not by the idea, only by the flippancy and brutality with which it is sometimes propounded.

At heart, their proposition is that it takes two people—a woman as well as a man—to have children; that the woman is not simply a vessel for an embryo that, designedly or inadvertently, has been planted by a man. Both man and woman must be at risk and in favor of what is happening. But the question that immediately follows is whether the principle is to work both ways—if the man as well as the woman is part of the equation and ought to be involved right through. Do single women, going beyond their power to terminate a pregnancy with or without the consent of the father, also have a moral right to initiate a pregnancy with an anonymously or carelessly donated vial of sperm, and then possibly flip out the fetus three months later, if they change their mind, their whim for self-fullfillment having meanwhile turned elsewhere? Some lesbians, in particular, welcome this additional freedom, but to my way of thinking, the welfare or the "rights" of the unborn may be more at hazard here than in the controversy over abortion itself, by which the unborn run the risk of never being born at all. In an imperfect world, many children are going to grow up without the benefit of two parents representing the two sexes, but they need not start out with fewer than two.

"Happiness is androgynous," as a heterosexual friend of mine was saying the other day. It must be so, because whenever one does see a grin of utter glee, or feel the same transfiguring smile of pleasure stretching one's own face, there is nothing "male" or "female" about the sensation. In real happiness, the lines of the face that distinguish us from one another by gender are erased; we become of the same race. But in attaining these epiphanies, we often need to leap the gap—one sex toward the other—for the sake of just this rich delight of compromising with one another.

"Strangely, laughter seems to me like the sexual act, which is perhaps the laughter of two bodies," says V. S. Pritchett. However, among feminists who neither wish to participate in the age-old, lifelong, gingerly, and rather exciting process of accommodation nor to become lesbians, there is a third course.

Oriana Fallaci's novel, *A Man*, revives a singularly innovative way of dealing with the continuing appeal of macho men: pick 'em wild and pick 'em doomed. Her brave Greek revolutionary, Alexander Panagoulis, is so far-out, frenetic, heroic, and self-destructive that it would be impossible for him ever to "tie her down." She can have her splendid romance without troubling to try to leap the gap because, in due course, he can only die, young and violently, freeing her from the necessity of making any compromising commitment to him, as well as from the likelihood that she will ever fall in love again. Who, after all, in raw maleness, could ever measure up to him? Nor need she wear a widow's weeds in a darkened drawing room, as women who loved mourning used to; she can roam the world as entrepreneur and parajournalist. And to be inseminated by such a hero would be ideal. In lovemaking, she has handled his war wounds and torture scars. He then departs the scene; and the lady, if she has a mind to, can marry her obliging, tidy-minded business manager for help in raising the twice-blest child.

As a program, it might prove popular, if enough heroes were at hand. It resembles the "hammer date" that Lenny Bruce liked to talk about in his monologues. A young stud wanted to screw, but he didn't want to have to hang around afterwards talking endlessly to his woman in return for her favors. So he got into bed with her, had his fuck, hit her over the head with the hammer, and went home.

This is an exaggeration. I meet women who wore jackboots and helped bust down the barriers at all-male saloons a decade ago, and who announce plaintively, ironically, to anybody listening that they "want to sue for peace," that they are marriageable, that with an amniocentesis it isn't yet too late for them to have a baby. Other women say they never *did* wear jackboots, that their opinions, if known, would be unfashionable among their sophisticated friends. And, of course, since even men in macho garb in fact are also greatly tamed (in backwoods America, too, if one puts one's ear close to the ground), conditions at the moment hint at a truce.

1980

A YEAR
AS IT TURNS

These seasonal editorials for *The New York Times* quite wrote themselves. I wanted them to, not being prepared to put as much regular effort into the job as Hal Borland had done during his thirty-seven-year stint on this newsman's beat—which ended with his death in 1978. Nor did the new *Times*, though personally hospitable and ready for stylistic innovation, wish for as much "nature" from me. I'd loved Borland's stuff; used to clip out of the Sunday paper his unsigned pieces that said spring slipped north sixteen miles and wound up a mountainside one hundred vertical feet in a day. Summer soul that I was, I'd sit in my New York apartment in April, impatiently calculating what I must be missing at my house in Vermont, which is eighteen hundred feet higher and three hundred eighty-four miles (by road) away. Perhaps unfortunately, I've been less informative, more contrapuntal than he.

I soon came to enjoy thinking up my own offerings and phoning them in from a booth on the highway. Since I was two miles from the nearest electricity, most were written in the evening by kerosene. Nevertheless, the voice here is institutional as well as individual, "moderate" and anonymous as well as idiosyncratic. Though it is a voice too cheerful, I've not tried to change these editorial statements into something more personal or polemical than the *Times* wanted to print under its own name, because I think that the attempt would wind up as a halfway measure, less satisfactory than these obvious hybrids, which already have a tradition in their original form.

But in some ways this is all by the by. None of us—not the *Times* with its bully pulpit nor *The New Yorker* in its editorial "we," not Hal Borland, E. B. White, Roger Tory Peterson, Annie Dillard, Edward Abbey, Peter Matthiessen, John McPhee, nor I—have been able to face up to the holocaust that is steadily consuming the natural world. Mr. Abbey walks, Mr. McPhee canoes, I write about animals, Mr. Matthiessen about birds. Yet we all know firsthand that the world we so dearly care about is tumbling around our ears. Activists from the past like John Muir and Rachel Carson would have been equally stunned at the earthwide scale.

In 1980 a presidential commission of scientists from eleven government agencies forecast that at least half a million species of plants and animals—one-fifth of Creation—will be destroyed in the next twenty years. Such an event of unspeakable magnitude, portending larger events, which may be observed in miniature by an educated traveler almost anywhere, can be forecast and partly reported. But we have the imperfect analogy of past holocausts as evidence that it can't be surrounded and dealt with by the mind of any one writer, until possibly later, when the worst is over and at last, in his humble inadequacy, he or his successors can begin to mourn what was lost.

JANUARY

WALKING THE DOG

WE ARE IN FAVOR of cleaning up after them, but we are also in favor of dogs. Manhattan was once the home of whistling swans and seals and mountain lions, and, walking the dog, we remember this in our bones. Walking a dog, we feel occasionally that we are with a living ancestor, as children seem to do also. Children are born with a liking for dogs; and when we are out with the family dog, we seem to remember aptitudes of nose and leg that we no longer have.

For the dog, one purpose of our walks is checking out the gutter—the chicken knuckles and Reuben sandwiches there. As a student of fermentation (wine and cheese buffs have nothing on him), he is immensely cheerful as we go around the block. Also, he marks his territory. You might say it's like the trappings of wolf territoriality without the territory, just as for us it is a walk in the woods without the woods. He looks particularly for irregularities to mark: a shovelful of dirt next to a Con Ed excavation, a clump of grass, houseplants or Christmas trees that have been thrown out but still smell of earth. Males found females by the process, but the other social function—when dogs were wolves—was to reinforce the order of rank and rule within the pack, increasing the pack's efficiency on a hunt.

We are animals too. We confront a cold wind with our backs, and turn grumpy if somebody unexpectedly grabs hold of us while we are bent over a steak. But the spirit of both man and dog is sociable, and most people will never be too old to get a kick out of whistling to a dog and seeing him wag his tail. The point of having a descendant of the Lost Wolf for company is not to crush his spirit but rather to direct it so that he can live in, even delight in, the city. The eagles and wild swans are gone, and we have an idea that dogs and the saving irregularities they look for add life to New York City.

FEBRUARY

STUTTERING TIME

WE HAVE A FRIEND who stutters; and while he notices no increase in rudeness or sarcasm from people in person, he does hear more impatience from telephone operators, secretaries, businessmen, switchboard personnel, and other strangers whom he must deal with over the phone. As he stands at a phone booth or holds on to the devilish device at home, the time allotted to him to spit out the words seems to have markedly shrunk; perhaps it has been halved in the past half-dozen years. This alarms him because at the same time the importance of the telephone in daily transactions has zoomed. Indeed, many people use answering machines to consolidate their calls, and soon voiceprinting may become a commonplace method of identification. Imagine, he suggests, stuttering into a voiceprinting machine.

Bell System operators, who used to be the most patient people he encountered, now often seem entirely unfamiliar with his handicap. They either hang up or switch him to their supervisors as a "problem call" after listening for only a few seconds, interrupting a couple of times to demand that he "speak clearly, please." They seem automated themselves, as if rigged to a stop clock that regulates how long they will listen to anything out of the ordinary, though twenty years ago, he says, they practiced their trade with a fine humanity.

But it is not just individuals in individual occupations who have changed. The division between personal life and business life has deepened, and the brusqueness of business gets worse all the time. At the bank, one can no longer choose one's teller but must stand in a single line. (The tellers seem to work more slowly, having less responsibility individually for the length of the line.) And inevitably, as we all become known more and more by account numbers, doing business will become still more impersonal, and any voice that doesn't speak as plainly as digits entering a computer will cause problems.

We have no solutions to offer. We have brought up the subject only because our friend sometimes feels like the canary that miners used to carry into a mine. He believes his increasing discomfort foretells a worsening shortness of breath in other people—even those who started out with no handicaps at all.

THE COST
OF FUR

WITH THE RECENT BOOM in "fun" furs—long-haired, wild-caught furs—prices paid to the trapper have gone up as much as 50 percent over last year, when they were already considered high. In the cold country of Glover, Vermont, for example, the local buyer has paid $38 for a top raccoon skin, versus $25 a year ago. Red foxes now range from $15, for a poor pelt, up to $77, versus $15 to $58 last year. Top eastern coyotes have gone to $50, and fishers to a high of $165.

But the water-living mammals, with shorter fur that doesn't impede their swimming and affords less "fun" to the final purchaser, have brought the trapper about the same price as he was getting before. Top Vermont wild mink are still worth no more than $25 or so; a good average muskrat, $5; a top otter, $65; and a "superblanket" beaver (one measuring over sixty-five inches when length and width of skin are added together), only $25.

In the impoverished north country, where a factory job is likely to pay just $20 a day after taxes, Al Brooks, the fur buyer in Glover, himself believes that prices for long-haired beasts have climbed too high. Every armchair cowboy who sees a hungry fox digging for mice in a snow-covered field is likely to grab a deer rifle and blast away, half ruining the pelt in the process, or will try to run over the animal on the road.

On the whole, however, wildlife is doing pretty well in Vermont's ninety-six hundred square miles. State biologists estimate a population of seventeen hundred bears, twelve hundred bobcats, one thousand coyotes, one hundred thousand deer, and even fifty moose—to mention a few relatively glamorous creatures. There have been worries about the bobcat—which furriers have been trying to promote into an alternative to the old superstylish leopard coat—and about a deer herd decreasing statewide because it had got out of balance with its winter forage. The deer will probably rebound, but the survival of bobcats, raccoons, foxes, and fishers depends not so much on a special food supply as on what's chic in New York City and Europe, and so is less certain.

MARCH

IN THE SPRING

In the spring fewer tankers steam into New York harbor, but more cruise ships are seen. The lobstermen set their pots in Gravesend Bay, just seaward of the Verrazano Bridge, and the flounder boats begin going out again. In Hoboken, on the Hudson, boys fish for blue crabs with killifish strung on a bait ring held over a net. The harbor is getting cleaner; there are even rumors that the defunct old oyster beds behind the Statue of Liberty have been showing signs of life.

On a ferryboat leaving the Battery, the passengers quickly step out on deck. The trees in Greenwood Cemetery in Brooklyn, on the ridge behind Gowanus Bay, are starting to green up. The prevailing wind is shifting southwesterly toward its summer slant. The deckhands on the tugboats are chipping off rust and painting red lead over the winter's wear and tear. Some tugs go into dry dock in Kill Van Kull to have their bottoms scraped and their propellers replaced after the chores of icebreaking.

From as far as Mount Marcy in the Adirondacks, three hundred miles away, the spring freshets sweep downriver, smelling like turtles as the weather warms. The Hudson has turned muddy as a frontier river—the rope fenders slung on the bow of each tug look like beaver skins—but the strong flow scrubs most of the winter sludge out of the harbor, leaving the water fresher and greener.

In the spring, sugar and coffee and banana boats sailing up from the tropics will carry a few vivid little birds, hitchhiking on their housing. They are canary-colored, red or orange—land birds that somehow got blown off course and lost at sea. Others may have died on the deck from exhaustion, but these found pools of rainwater and are alive.

In the city, too, rare birds—like mimes and mouth organists and three-card-shuffling mountebanks—emerge from cellar hideaways and perform in the streets. Another cold winter survived.

MARCH

CHIAROSCURO

Observing that dimming the lights at his daughter's tenth birthday party reduced the level of squabbling considerably, a man we know was reminded of his own good cheer when

he steps into the dim illumination of a bar in his neighborhood. In weaker lighting, both his cantankerousness and
some of his inhibitions fall away. He even becomes a bit of
an actor. He can lie a little, on days when it seems to ease
the heart to stretch the truth, or may pretend to be happier or unhappier, younger or older than he really is. Wearing his choice of a drink like a favorite hat, he compares
Harry ("The Cat") Brecheen's pitching tricks with Catfish Hunter's, talking to a patent attorney who remembers
only the latter.

His grandmother distrusted bright electricity too. She
used to tell how kerosene lamps had strained her eyes when
she was a child, and still preferred to read by natural light,
even on a cloudy afternoon—then put her book aside to
converse at dusk. Our friend, on the other hand, being a
creature of the electric age, feels funny if he finds himself
reading by any source other than a light bulb. If a shaft of
sunlight falls on the page, he feels he should be up and
about and out of doors.

Yet while he tends not to tell lies in broad daylight, or
launch into a disquisition on Brecheen's screwball before
sundown, his fancy and his memory do operate in the sunshine. When he is hurrying to an appointment, preparing to
cross the street against the traffic, he sometimes finds himself taking a lead off first base, just the way his high school
coach taught him to do. The sun pours on him and he rocks
on his feet, ready to dash to second or to spring back safely
to the curb.

Especially as the winter blurs into earliest spring, the sun
begins to soothe him and set his imagination simmering. It's
a time of year when he may step into his neighborhood tav-
ern but then set foot outside again, standing in the doorway
to catch the last evening rays full on his face.

LOVE
STORY

PEOPLE IN THE COUNTRY celebrate spring by picking wild leeks in the woods for salad and soup. In Greenwich Village a man with a conch shell walks out on the Bank Street Pier and blows his greetings to the *QE2* as she slides down the Hudson, hoping she'll answer with an ocean-deep toot. On a warm windy day everybody outside wears a bit of a grin. Riding the ferry to Staten Island, a boy scrutinizes his girlfriend's back teeth, while combing her hair with his hand, in a trance of love.

Not just gulls are riding the garbage barges; a few cattle egrets are back from the South to pick up what they can. In the wholesale meat market around Gansevoort Street there are gulls on the sidewalk, and gulls on the pretty blue roof of the fireboat pier at the Battery.

But pigeons are busier, romancing. With their croony croak, their street minuet performed on red, lizard legs, pigeons are the birds of spring in the city. They fly like cliff-nesters adept at dodging a merlin, and are feeders of opportunity. Another adaptation that long predates cities but fits them for life in the metropolis is that they don't feed their squabs litter straight out of the gutter. Rather, both parents predigest the litter and manufacture "pigeon's milk," which is a curdlike, white, almost mammalian substance, triggered by the hormone prolactin and chemically resembling rabbit's milk, but formed of rapidly growing cells on the walls of the crop that are sloughed off and regurgitated into the infant's mouth. Though pigeons, which lay only a couple of eggs at a stint, run out of milk in about ten days, they've given their young a head start.

So when we see pigeons puff up their chests as they circle and strut, perhaps, besides courting, they are expanding their crops. And that whimsical man who goes out on the pier with his conch shell, instead of into the woods after leeks, is making his own happy adjustment to spring in the city.

APRIL

THERE GO THE CLOWNS

THE WORD "CLOWN" probably derives from *klunni*, which meant "loutish" in Old Norse. There have been three kinds of clowns. The white-faces had sunny, quick, boyish souls. The pink-and-red-and-white "august" clowns were foolish guys, bumpkins, scapegoats, and stuffed shirts. The character clowns, playing cops, farmers, ethnics, and so on, depended upon costuming and frequently wore darker makeup to add complexity to their temperament.

In America the best character clowns were two hoboes invented during the Depression by Emmett Kelly and his good friend Otto Griebling. Kelly, who died in Florida last Wednesday, wore blackish, reddish, grayish makeup on his cheeks and chin, white and black on his mouth, and a polka-dot derby. He was broke and sad and seedy—in short, a tramp. Griebling projected an angrier, "crazier" idea of humanity and of those times, but both were men for the 1930s, not for our more prosperous, fast-paced decade. Slow in all his movements, Emmett Kelly would fall in love with ladies in the crowd, turn out his ragged pockets, weep unashamedly at supposed slights—none of which we like to see ourselves as doing, lately. He would hit a peanut with a sledgehammer, or juggle while balancing a feather on the tip of his nose.

There is a dearth of clowns today. Ringling Bros. and Barnum & Bailey has had to establish a Clown College to fill its need for replacements, and almost all the young talent is either white-faced or "august." They wear painted overalls or neon suits. Though nothing is wrong with that, we miss the tramps. And we will particularly miss "Weary Willie"—Emmett Kelly's creation—for his leisurely sweetness and his vulnerability.

APRIL

MOUNTAIN HOUSE

THE STARTLING, LOOMING BARNS, the intricate profusion of trees along the highway; then a dirt road winding up through woods, past melting banks of snow, to the notch of a mountain, where fields open out—all so newly marvelous to city eyes that it seems almost too good to be true that the house itself is still standing, ready for another summer's use.

A week after Easter, snow is waist-high under the roof, but the fields are nearly bare. Two crows are eating thawing apple pulp under a tree just in back. A red-tailed hawk is cruising overhead, swimming upward in the thermals. The deer, which winter in a cedar swamp a couple of miles downhill, have not yet shown up, but a bear, incautious as always in the early spring, has made straight for the pond below the fields on the same path that fishermen will soon be using. There is also an otter's track; and a white snowshoe rabbit that the foxes didn't catch during the winter is already speckled with summer brown. The bear himself is a survivor. Hunters working through with a pack of hounds in the fall killed three other bears on the mountain.

A freight train derailed in town, and the usual scattering of winter bankruptcies disrupted people's peace of mind. Nowadays it happens mostly to newcomers from New Jersey whom the native Vermonters have conned into buying defunct general stores. But everybody has stopped to take stock, looking around to see who else has lasted out the snowbound months without turning into a drunk.

It has been an uncertain maple-sugaring season—March's weather like April, and April's like March. But people are buying seed potatoes to plant, and digging last year's parsnips out of the ground. Parsnips, with a white, knotty-looking, carrotlike taproot, were a favorite vegetable among the pioneers. They winter in the garden as well as a bear does in his cave, and aren't just hardy—they actually sweeten there; they make better eating in the spring for the experience of overwintering.

SWAMP
ENSEMBLE*

PEEPERS HIBERNATE AMONG ROOTS and under moss; wood frogs, in the punk of stumps or under logs; toads, in burrows under rocks and boards. But the spring releases all of them, as everywhere the water flows. Spring *is* water, and the streams turn brown, with duck tracks in the mud, old leaves shining like turtle shells. Leopard and pickerel frogs have hibernated under stones in brooks where the water ran too fast to freeze, but they, too, head for the pond.

The peepers sing in a ringing, monotonous, fitfully exhilarating call. Inch-sized, with x's on their backs, they seem to be in residence in every country neighborhood for a few weeks. The wood frogs congregate in woodside pools, where they cluck quite clamorously, like chickens falling on top of one another. The spotted leopard frogs converse with a snoring croak or rattle, and pickerel frogs with a sound like cloth ripping, before laying their eggs and heading for the meadowlands again.

Native to the pond are the green frogs—which have wintered on the bottom wedged between stones so that they wouldn't float up—as well as their large, less adventurous look-alikes, the bullfrogs, which merely dig down in the mud. Green frogs croak explosively, but bullfrogs calmly announce, "Be drowned. Better go 'round," as we stand on the bank looking at them.

---

*This editorial, and "December Song," appeared in *The Nation*, not the *Times*.

A bullfrog takes a year to emerge from the tadpole stage, and, ever after, an extra month to arouse in the spring. But toads—quicker to metamorphose, wider-ranging—are kings of the Batrachians, one might say. With their proverbial sparkling eyes—which, like a magician's, are employed also in spooning down a hefty mouthful when suddenly retracted into the head—and with their changes of color several times a day, their habit of bursting out of and swallowing their skins, toads are a triumph of mystery and versatility. Like a magician, a toad fights off its enemies with secretions of the skin. Turn-of-the-century violinists, indeed, are said to have rubbed their hands on an obliging toad before a performance because these poisons prevented their fingers from slipping.

MAY

THE
BITTERN
BOOMETH

THERE'S NOTHING LIKE A CANOE. A friend in New England recently put in an asparagus bed he won't be able to enjoy a meal from for two years. Also spinach for this summer, onions for the fall, Jerusalem artichokes for a Christmas treat —but he was ready for some pleasure now; and that's what his canoe was for.

Right away on the river, he heard a mating snipe flinging itself about the sky in order to impress its female, with a faint laughing ululation such as children make when hooting with their hands in front of their mouths. He saw some sandpipers, or "teeter-tails," tipping up their tails as they searched for invertebrates. A gray marsh hawk seized a dazed and chilly frog before his eyes, and half a dozen geese were still dawdling south of their nesting ground in passionate but wary pairs.

The skunk cabbage was as vivid a green as anything in sight, and the river flowed like a tale being told for a thousand years. Although he has some doubts about what the next thousand will be like, he met a bittern on the lookout for crayfish and sounding its slow, pumping "pile driver's" cry, *oong-KA-choonk! oong-KA-choonk!* When he paddled closer, the bird raised its bill straight up until its tall brown body blended with the reeds, even swaying slightly, like the reeds in the wind.

Chaucer's Wife of Bath says that "a bittern boometh in the quagmire," and so this secretive heron gave him a double kind of cheer—that he was hearing the same salutation Chaucer heard six hundred years ago, and that two years seemed not so long to wait before he could begin eating his asparagus.

MAY

SONGS
AND
SNAKESKINS

SPRING MAKES NEARLY every creature exuberant, it seems. A friend, canoeing in Vermont, noticed a granddaddy snapping turtle, as big as a washtub, swimming alongside his craft for possibly a mile, with a curiosity the turtle no doubt is going to lose after a few more canoeists go by. A bear emerges to graze the tender meadow grass in his back field as early as 5:00 P.M., and the cow moose that likes to eat pond weeds in the marsh downhill from him can hardly be scared away before eight in the morning—these being the daylight feeding hours that moose and bear preferred before they had so many human neighbors to contend with.

Spring is the time when beasts stoke up after the hardships of the winter, and when birds court a mate and stake a territory. Some of the most beautiful birdsongs are contentious in intent. The flicker's speedy, bouncing flight as it crosses a clearing to pound its bill on a dead limb, the woodcock's yo-yo courtship display, spiraling high and plummeting—these are part of the inimitable panache of spring. Yet how can one explain the search great crested flycatchers make for a snakeskin to weave into the lining of their nests? Where snakeskins have become hard to obtain, they substitute a scrap of cellophane. The bird is only robin-sized, but surely a seasonal and talismanic exuberance is involved here.

Our friend must scratch his blackfly bites, which also go with spring, and sometimes will wake up at 3:00 A.M. to a dead, wintry chill. He loads wood into the stove and reassures himself that he is on the younger side of middle age and, furthermore, that this is May. With dawn, the vireos and song sparrows strike up and say indeed it's so.

COMPLEX
JUSTICE

CHIPPING SPARROWS LIKE TO LINE their nests with horsehair. If a farmer has no horses, they will sometimes pull hair for the purpose out of his cow dog as it sleeps in the yard.

The spring rains make a lovely din on his tin roof after the snowy silence of the winter. Rain brings up his hay and pasture grasses quickly, but torrents of rain may rot his seed corn and potatoes and make it difficult for him to maneuver his tractor and corn planter. (Sometimes he thinks the sparrows are right to wish he still kept horses.)

Rain also brings out the horseflies and deerflies. Yet with the flies come the swallows that nest in the farmer's barn and swirl outside, clocking as much as six hundred miles a day in sweeps and zigzags, as if the sky were an ocean to sport in. At corn-planting time a flock of crows arrives to raid his fields for seed, but the swallows—with nests to defend—take out after the crows and drive them away.

The farmer, who has "buried his money for the summer," as he likes to say when he has plowed in store-bought fertilizer, appreciates the complicated justice of all this. If the flies weren't biting him he wouldn't have swallows, and if he didn't have swallows the crows would grab more of his corn. However, he only grows corn to feed his cows next winter, when there will be no flies around and the swallows will be in South America. So if he didn't keep cows he wouldn't need the corn, and wouldn't have either the problem of the crows that raid his fields or the clouds of flies drawn to his barn. The swallows then could stay in

South America, and he'd just have a few sparrows picking nest hairs off his sleeping collie, and maybe a few pretty tiger swallowtail butterflies clustered around the mud puddles in front of his empty barn.

But *that* would be no way to try to raise a family.

JUNE

TUG OF
SWEET TROUT

JUNEBERRIES ARE AMONG the earliest wild fruits. In pioneer times they were also named serviceberries, because their white blossoms bloomed almost as soon as the ground thawed and a family that had been saving a body through icy weather to bury when the ground turned soft could cover the grave with these first flowers. Woods blossoms like trout lilies come nearly as early, in order to crowd the best of life into the few brief weeks between the time when the soil thaws and the growth of a full canopy of trees blocks out the sun. And trout—and fishermen—are active too, now that the confining cap of ice is off the ponds and a skyful of food is falling on the water.

Of course, the fish don't stop eating with the end of spring. Nor do our fishing friends quit angling for them with a whole miniature circus procession of gaudy flies that week by week approximate the cycles of insect life until midsummer. Where fishing pressure is heavy, the smarter anglers have listened carefully during the spring for frog songs originating in unexpected directions. Beavers may have constructed a new pond, which the frogs and trout discover. The fisherman who follows may find a spring peeper in the stomach of the first fat trout he catches. In a sense, therefore, with his game fish, he's eating flies and frogs.

But frogs' legs are an expensive delicacy; and little wild woods flies taste sweet, as any fair-minded person knows who has had one fly into his mouth and has stopped to analyze, after spitting it out, what he is tasting. In any case, most people fish not for the sweetness of the trout so much as for the tug—a tug that comes from the netherworld of mayflies, trout lilies, juneberries, and spring frogs.

JUNE

THE
PRIME
OF LIFE

COTTON FLUFF IS BLOWING from the poplar trees on the mountainside. Chokecherries and wild strawberries are in blossom, and a flock of goldfinches has gathered to pick apart the dandelions. The porcupines are on the move, from the ledgy spruce forest where they wintered to juicy fields and toothsome orchards. At night an owl yaps at the dog and at dawn the warblers and the redstarts make the woods ring. A grouse is drumming, sounding like someone unsuccessfully cranking an outboard motor.

It is the time of year when one's best possession is one's

legs. A wanderer can fish the culverts or nibble sorrel in the woods. Around an old cellar hole there are purple lilacs and moss phlox, apple trees covered with flowers, and a row of maples swelling as big as goons in silhouette against the sky. A pair of nesting ravens somewhere up along the cliffs croaks incessantly. They feel so inaccessible they don't mind betraying their position. Even two Vermont coyotes, intent on not giving away the location of their pups, can't help gabbling at each other for a second in the excitement of the season.

At the pond a dozen salamanders are feeding on an ice-killed fish. The trees, fighting for sun, jam their boughs together. They used to meet in an arcade above the road, but there are fewer tall ones now. With the pinch in fuel-oil prices, a tradition of New England democracy has been revived: trees along backcountry roads belong to whoever has a cold house. The climate is tough, and yet the ringing, rapid-fire birdsongs prove that here in the north is where all these hosts of migrators prefer to breed. They want the blackflies, and the seeds pulled from the poplar fluff. They fly here for the prime of life.

JUNE

IN THE
WOODS

A friend in the country with a woodlot at his disposal points out that even in the summer all this stored-up sunshine does him good. His woodpile helps to keep him fed

187

because the rich soil underneath is the best place to dig fishing worms; and every June he sets up a small tent in the woods at the edge of a field, where, surrounded by goosefoot, bull thistle, and fir trees, he can spend the full-moon nights and other moments when the spirit moves.

The tent seems to breathe in the wind. It's always ready for him, with a sleeping bag and an air mattress full of his own hot breath on the ground. He goes out after any storm to guy the ropes snugly again, as if for the comfort of his alter ego, and will dawdle there an hour among the timberdoodles and the teacher birds. A tree swallow darts high with a feather, drops it deliberately, then swoops to catch it again. A woodchuck is raising a family in her summer den —not the same den that she hibernated in; that's back in the woods, headquarters for a skunk family now. Once when the woodchuck sat up close to his tent, as brindled-brown and husky-torsoed as a grizzly bear, he thought he might be camping in Alaska—except that, at the same time, a catbird overhead was mimicking the song of some Southern bird that the catbird, too, may have heard in Georgia last winter.

Many nights an owl flies to a tree overlooking the field and, after a watchful moment, hoots for an answer from another owl—although for want of a better interlocutor, it sometimes converses with him. His knowledge of the language of barred owls is rudimentary, but the eight-beat calls end with a sort of doggish bark. So for a few minutes he and the owl say back and forth something like "*Whooo cooks for you? Whooo cooks for you-ALL?*"

JUNE

NORTH COUNTRY DIARY

BIG BLUE CLOUDS, then mare's tails in the sky, the brook in perpetual motion. It's haying week in the north country, and a mowing machine decades old seems to do as good a job as anything newer. Afterward the cows are let into the stubble, where deer join them in the evening, protesting like a trumpet sneezing if the farmer interrupts them. The deer have turned from winter-gray to summer-red, and woodchucks that were as thin as rats in April have fattened magisterially.

The fireflies are bluish white—star-colored. A bullfrog has eaten so many that he himself begins to glow. Bullfrogs wrestle in the pond for breeding territory, or lie like wishbones in the shallows. A woodpecker bangs the metal roof of the barn to announce his presence. Grouse, and even wood ducks, moving around in search of food, have brought their babies out beside the road. And there are bats at night; throw up a pebble and they go for it.

The highbush cranberries are in flower—and oxeye daisies, lemon lilies, lady's slippers, blue flag, blackberry blossoms, pasture roses, sarsaparilla, cow parsnips, and columbine. Two hummingbirds take turns perching on the top twig of an apple tree, surveying all these flowers. Butterflies visit the hawkweed with a staggered flight to evade pursuers, but one after another, a phoebe grabs them. The

189

grosbeaks peck impatiently at raspberries scarcely past flowering.

A screech owl whinnies like a muted loon. A loon wails like a lobo wolf. A fox barks. Transferring her pups to a new den, she will carry along their favorite toys also—a jay's foot, a weasel's skull. Just at the summer solstice the night was short and moonless. But first the stars and then the dawn were brighter for it.

STARS TO EAT

Two country axioms are that the last run of maple sap comes at the same time that the first spring frogs start to peep, and that wild strawberries are ripe to pick when the summer's fireflies flash their lights. Suddenly this has become the case, and there are sweets to gather in the fields. The fireflies themselves are sweets to frogs—a firmament of stars to eat. Once the frogs have laid their eggs, they have no further duties except to fatten up.

The deer are fat as clams. The foxes have begun to teach their pups to hunt. Chanticleer, strutting around in the dooryard, must watch his step—although it sometimes seems as if the reason roosters have been endowed with such splendid necks is not to see over the grass to spot a fox but only so they can look around at their tall tails. In fuss and feathers, as they hunt for a grasshopper, they resemble many human beings.

We have friends who spend all summer oiling themselves at the beach, and friends who garden busily behind the house—they've already eaten their rhubarb and are starting in on their Bibb lettuce. Peerless salad makers, these are people who in the spring will line the kitchen windowsill with pots of cauliflower and broccoli, instead of flowering plants. In September they will set a dozen ripening tomatoes there.

It's been said that in the summer we all fall into one of two groups: beach people or mountain people. We hope to receive invitations for the weekend from both kinds. And in fairness to the rooster and to all who resemble him, we should add that it is not just he who crows so proudly each summer dawn; it is the whole world of birds.

JULY

୬‖‖ଛ

SUMMER
POND

SWIMMING IN A SUMMER POND, we notice how natural it is to use all four limbs to travel along. We are a quadruped again; even the stroke we do is called "the crawl." Opening our eyes underwater, we look down instead of straight ahead or up. A log sunk on the bottom looms like a snapping turtle. The stems of the pond lilies, rising five feet, tangle one's arms a little frighteningly—people have sometimes drowned that way—and leeches live among them, eating bullfrogs' eggs. But a porcupine will happily swim out to chew the lily pads, just as a beaver may climb the bank to eat raspberries for a change of fare.

Out deeper, in cooler water, where trout live, floating on one's back is a kind of free ride, like being fifteen again, like being afloat upon another sky. We turn and lapse into a dead man's float. Perhaps there is a bit of Tom Sawyer's pleasure at watching his own bogus funeral in this, but before we get overly morbid, a fish begins nibbling our toes. Floating on one's back is like riding between two skies. And then we do the crawl in a predatory manner again, watching for trout below—moving like a tiger in our mind's eye, forepaws padding up and down. We lose our poise, however, as soon as we remember the big snapping turtle that might be drifting underneath us in the muddy gloom.

Of course the snapping turtle has her nemesis too—the skunks that every year dig her eggs out of the sand. There is a complex citizenship to the natural world that we are a part of when we swim. We have no special human powers, no superior dispensation, then. In its mystery, its profound and changeable reverberations in both the memory and the mind, swimming is a decathlon all by itself. We love it as we love to walk and run—and in the summer, maybe more.

AUGUST

THE
ROAR OF
THE MOON

BEAVERS OCCASIONALLY WILL CLIMB out of a pond at the height of the summer and stretch out comfortably in the sun on an anthill to let the ants clean the gunk out of their fur. Maybe such pleasures of the season make them feel expansive, just as we do, lying under the summer sun and gazing at a spruce tree upside down.

Summer is when we look for ostrich ferns, bearhead mushrooms, and clouded sulphur butterflies. It's a time when, at the beach listening to the roar of the tide, we remember that what we're really hearing is the roar of the moon. Summer is when we believe, all of a sudden, that if we just walked out the back door and kept on going long enough and far enough we would reach the Rocky Mountains.

Anyway, if we get no farther than a weekend in New Hampshire, we like our mountains with some clouds swirling about them, and like to hear a rain squall spatter against the tent. It's cozier; and the clouds, by partly hiding the mountains, lend them an extra dimension. They seem to soar higher because their shapes are not entirely defined. We can imagine we are in Montana—or, in Montana, that we are in Nepal.

We burn marshmallows, pick brown-eyed Susans, and eat sweet corn, and think of other summers when we had a very special love affair, or canoed a hundred miles, or journeyed into Canada and saw a wolf.

IN
THE PAWS
OF THE SURF

TOSSING IN THE PAWS of the surf under a buttery sunset at the end of the summer, it is pleasant to suppose that one really is at that moment a plaything of the sea. The few dangers, like jellyfish or an undertow, are not hard to deal with if one has chosen one's beach and one's day. On such an occasion nature seems luscious indeed, or tamed.

Even seamen now speak of crossing the Atlantic as "crossing the pond," and weathermen, interpreting satellite photographs on TV, wear feathery hairdos, as if they had never stepped out-of-doors and felt any rain. Farming, too, has been mechanized and our other conquests over nature have accelerated to such a degree that we forget that a nuclear catastrophe, more than an old-fashioned war fought with gunpowder, could simply become nature functioning in the biggest way. We forget that hyperactive sexuality and big-league sporting events represent only a rearrangement of aboriginal energies that otherwise remain dormant in us until such time as primeval conditions may call them forth in an undisguised state.

Peregrine falcons are hunting pigeons over Central Park once again; and anybody who keeps chickens knows that although it is seldom possible for hens to brood their own eggs nowadays, if given a chance some of them will enter a fuguelike state and happily do so. The pigs that are being raised on factory farms without enough space to turn around in, if let loose, would still be the smartest animals in the barnyard.

Under hard conditions nature endures. No matter where you store a potato—under the dankest sink—its eyes will sprout. Most of the saucing and seasoning of food that we do only parallels the piquancy fermentation lends to the "kills" other predators eat. And it behooves us to remember that we are a part of nature and that its strength vastly surpasses our own. Especially in a nuclear age, we bob in the paws of the surf in January as well as the balmy summertime.

SEPTEMBER

FIRE WORSHIPER

We know a man who bought his first orange at a county fair for a nickel, having walked barefoot from home, carrying his shoes. The closest thing to a machine on the midway was the horse that tugged the merry-go-round around. Honest-to-goodness Gypsies told your fortune and a few Indian families selling baskets came over from Maine.

At the fair now, the teamsters still have a chance to show what their big pulling horses did in the woods all last winter. There are competitions of harvest vegetables and knitted afghans, a milk-cow cavalcade, a promenade of antique cars, a sideshow tent with a Fire Worshiper, a genuine Blockhead, even an advertised Creole Woman. Then, after Fair Week, people start laying in firewood and banking the house for winter all over again.

From spring peepers to autumn crickets, the year speeds by. Scarlet tanagers, molting for winter, are already dappled with green. Bluejays, having gorged on enough blueberries (it seems) to keep them blue for the rest of the year, are feasting on acorns; and at the edge of the forest, orange-flowered jewelweed is a favorite food for both the bears and hummingbirds.

A garter snake will shed about three skins during the summer, growing each new one to fit its increased size. So though the snake goes blind for several days, there is a triumph to the process—not like the dropping of leaves from a tree. Unfortunately, we're more like the tree. When we put off our summer skin it means we are a year older, not bigger and better, and cold winds lie ahead.

But we need to remind ourselves that Labor Day is only a holiday, not the beginning of the fall. A month of summery weather is left. The geese, not Congress, will mark the proper change of season.

SEPTEMBER

DEADLY COLORS

TREE SWALLOWS LIKE to stick a white feather upright at the back of their nests, in a dark cozy hole high in a tree, to help them navigate as they swoop in to land at dusk. Possibly it also gives a cheerful cast to the coming of the night—much as bright fall colors ease us into accepting the winter's short cold days and indoor life. Whole hills of sugar maples turn rose-colored, and three weeks later, as if to wind things up, the larches go all gold.

When the maples turn, August's chokecherry wine is ready to drink (unless you'd prefer it to taste more like sherry than like cherry), and the mushroom season ends. Mushrooming is no more dangerous than highway driving, as long as you know the colors on which life-and-death decisions depend. Carrot-colored milk mushrooms, yellow-orange chanterelles, off-white oyster mushrooms, creamy meadow mushrooms, and the toasty-brown Boletus species are delicious when sautéed—unless you have confused them with a deadly look-alike which will put you in your grave posthaste.

The poisonous and nonpoisonous varieties of the genus Amanita range from white and vivid lemon-yellow through shades like opera pink and old olive to brilliant scarlet. Most have a pretty ruffled skirt somewhere along the stem and an intriguing stippled effect on the cap, as though rock salt had been sprinkled there.

You can cash in your chips by eating an Amanita "toadstool" by mistake. So when the autumn leaves, in purples, reds and yellows, skate gently down and cover all the brown and red and orange mushrooms—greenish "death cap," creamy "poison pie," and white "destroying angel," as well as the savory vermilion and golden chanterelles that are so good to eat—we feel some relief. Certain risks, decisions and ways of living high and dangerously have been postponed until next spring.

✳

LABELS
VERSUS
LIFE

READING A SECTION about turtles in Thoreau's journals, we noticed that several of the Latin or Greek scientific names he used have changed. *Emys*, the genus name for painted turtles, has become *Chrysemys*. *Cistuda*, box turtles, are now *Terrapene*. *Chelonura*, snapping turtles, are *Chelydra*. Many creatures' Latin names, although intended by their originators to stand immutable, do seem to alter faster than the common English ones, as later scientists reorganize taxonomy. And after affixing a Latin name, too many scientists thought that the wild animal or plant itself would remain as indestructible as they imagined their choice of Latin to be.

This past summer for us has contained, as for Thoreau, an intricacy of broad-winged hawks and short-tailed weasels, cinnamon ferns and basswood trees, star-nosed moles and milk snakes, wild thyme and ground cedar, tamaracks and meadowsweet. We hope that summers always will. Certainly Thoreau's prose has outlasted scientific nomenclature, but even the most permanent prose has yet to prove its efficacy against, say, acid rain. We hope Thoreau's English does not outlast some of the forms of wildlife he was celebrating—what a heart-sickening outcome that would be.

Latin cognomens have one great function. They are for shouting across the barrier of languages and oceans. Our

198

wood warblers, red-eyed vireos, scarlet tanagers, kingbirds, northern orioles and indigo buntings, for example, winter in Latin American forest habitats that are being destroyed at a rate of at least one percent a year. Recent samplings indicate an alarming, correspondent shrinkage in the numbers of several migrant birds.

There is no simple solution, and no monopoly of concern north of the border. But we hope the international mails are humming on this matter, with lots of Latin names interspersing the Spanish and the English.

OCTOBER

BARKING GEESE AND BUTTERNUTS

LAST SPRING'S PIGS have grown so big they're already having trouble peering out from underneath their ears. Maples are turning carmine and coral, beech trees bronze, and blackberry leaves wine-dark. Poplars are slower to change because they try to squeeze every last growing day out of the year, but oaks are slow from being rather stately anyway; they're slow both in the fall and spring.

Birds have good mating or territorial reasons for flaunting a spectrum of colors (and tropical species, in their density, achieve the widest variety). But nobody quite knows why our Northern trees should turn such marvelous colors. As fall begins, the leaves have died to a singed green, obviously finished for the year. Then, unnecessarily, it would seem, they blazon into clarion reds and yellows that will appear in tiers on a steep hill, the maples lower, the birches higher—all looking best when set off by a sensible stand of firs that have remained dark green. It is a spectacle most lovely during a rare, premature snowfall.

Dairy farmers are chopping fields of feed corn for their cattle, now that the first frost has caught the sugar in the leaves and dried the leaves so that the juice won't sink into the roots or drain onto the silo floor. You can pick up butternuts in the woods, staining your fingers with the dye Confederate uniforms were tinted with, and see the laddering of fresh claw prints on large beech trees where the impatient bears have scrambled up to shake the beechnuts off the limbs.

Open a milkweed pod and look at the brown seeds, as neatly overlaid as feathers on a pheasant's back. The butterflies that ate the leaves are on their way to Mexico, but birds and beasts that have remained, at the same time as they're fattening for winter, must face the hunting season. Baying beagles and coonhounds hit the woods, sounding like that first flight of Canada geese that very shortly will speed overhead in an arrowy V, barking vigorously to each other.

So, it's flying season for the geese, fattening season for woodchucks, hunting season for the hounds, and rutting season for the moose. Moose have such long legs that, at least in our Eastern woods, they can winter wherever they like in the snow—halfway up a mountain as easily as down on a river bottom with the frailer deer. Wild dogs can't kill them—nothing but a poacher can—and when they want to nibble the buds on a small tree, they simply straddle it and ride it down.

OCTOBER

CITY
PEBBLES

JUST BACK FROM A COUNTRY SUMMER, we got all slicked up
in a suit and tie to walk the avenues, and very soon encountered a movie being filmed, a handsome pocket park with
crashing fountain, St. Patrick's Cathedral getting a face-
wash, and Central Park's noble landscaping, with larger
trees of more species than most woodsmen are used to. We
saw so many people, and *liked* so many people, it was exhilarating.

Like pebbles in a river, people in a great metropolis come
in more colors, shapes, and sizes than people elsewhere. And
yet, for all the talk of abrasive eccentricity rife in New
York City, we find people here, taken as a whole, more
rounded—probably from rubbing against each other—than
people in the country. "Sophistication" is another word for
that inventive mix of tolerance, resilience, and resourceful-
ness city people develop. They aren't necessarily subtler,
but they are more supple, which is why, against great odds
sometimes, they stay so sane.

We wouldn't for a moment deny the stamina and good
humor of country folk, who are the glue of the ages. But
our heart leaped up when we set foot on pavement again,
just as it had when we first plunged into the woods last
spring. The steel-drum combos, the walking stereos, the
businessman boasting sotto voce to his svelte companion, "I
have a national hookup from here to California," the nut
wearing gloves but no shoes—we liked it. City people think
life is short and is what you make of it. They believe that

you can alter life. Even more than stamina, they believe in
drama.

HEEL
AND TOE

A FRIEND OF OURS looks out on the West Side Highway,
downtown where it has been abandoned for vehicular use.
Only joggers, strolling lovers, heel-and-toe walkers, boxers
working out, and people running with their dogs are up
there now. A model gets her exercise while holding an umbrella over her head to avoid a burn, and several men who
might be Wall Street brokers run by with watches in hand,
much as they time themselves by the ticker tape the rest of
the day. Particularly curious is the slender, diminutive
figure who runs quite hard, like a professional (say, a circus
professional), juggling three red balls.

Our friend remembers the morning of the New York City
marathon last fall. There were fewer runners past his window; most were either entered in the race or cheering from
the sidelines. But that foggy October morning was the occasion when the first Canada geese came through on their
thousand-mile flight south. Honking, hollering to each
other, barking like hounds, they sped down the Hudson
just as their ancestors did when the Dutch first settled here
and the Hudson River was full of salmon, porpoises, and
otters. The astonished gulls who live along the piers took to
the air in whirling white lariats and in great alarm.

On the waterfront there are eel fishermen, prostitutes, and pushcart peddlers selling hot dogs. Perhaps the democracy of the sea affects them, they get along so well. The other day two actors were rehearsing Tybalt's duel with Romeo. And people come to where the land meets the water for special conversations. They can propose marriage; they can simply relax. Even when our friend is gloomy, the neighborhood cheers him up. He trapped a mouse the other day, a depressing event. But when he flushed it down the toilet, a speck of life leaped free and out. Say that it represented what you like. It was a flea.

NOVEMBER

RATTLESNAKE
STAKES

ONE MAN'S MEAT is another man's poison. But we suspect one reason why some of the he-man power brokers who dine at Dominique D'Ermo's gourmet restaurant in Washington, D.C., like to eat rattlesnakes is that in life the snakes were poisonous. A formerly dangerous creature sautéed in wine and safely tucked into the stomach makes them feel stronger and is something to boast about. Cannibals felt the same way about consuming an enemy. So do cowboys after a meal of "prairie oysters"—bull-calf testicles. Cecil Andrus, who, as Secretary of the Interior, is in charge of the endangered-species program, eats at Dominique's and says he "hates" rattlesnakes. He fired a scientist in his department who wrote the restaurateur to protest the menu listing of an Eastern-type rattler that is fast dwindling in numbers.

Secretary Andrus comes from Idaho, and it has not been long since some of that state's mountainmen were frying steaks cut out of cougars and grizzlies. Who's to say that, in their day, they shouldn't have? The trouble is that formerly dangerous creatures have a way of vanishing, just like creatures that are not dangerous. Rhinoceroses are endangered in Africa because rich Asians believe that powdered rhino horn prolongs male potency. Tigers in wildlife preserves in India have been cut down partly for their whiskers, which are reputed to possess comparable powers. On the other hand, several species of dolphin are in danger of disappearing because for years fishing boats have followed them to locate yellowfin tuna, which the dolphins eat, and have drowned thousands of dolphins as the tuna were netted. Great whales have been minced into margarine oil, cosmetics, and car lubricants to the point where many species have nearly perished.

Secretary Andrus is in favor of protecting dolphins, whales, even tigers, but he is quoted as finding it "humorous" that rare rattlesnakes might be worth protecting. Such a personal whim should not determine the fauna of the future. Snake venom is useful in cancer, antibiotic, and other medical research, and even if there were no practical considerations, a question would remain. Does Mr. Andrus or anyone else believe that it is more dangerous to allow small numbers of rattlesnakes to survive in remote areas than to trifle with the diversity of life itself on earth?

NOVEMBER

COLD MALES,
NEO-FEMALES

Audubon MAGAZINE REPORTS that nesting temperatures on the beach help to determine the sex of hatchling sea turtles. Warmer nests produce females; cooler nests, baby males. We were reminded that jack-in-the-pulpit plants tend to become male in years when undernourishment has left them weak, but female when local conditions have infused the same flower with renewed strength.

There are fish and shellfish that start life as males and later change into females, as if being female were indicative of maturity. The common toad, however, possesses a special, curious device called the Bidder's organ, which is present in both sexes close to the original genitalia. Though ordinarily it has no role, in case of a castrating injury it will promptly develop into a functioning ovary, even in adults that have previously fathered tadpoles. Such males become "neo-females," mating with normal males and laying eggs.

The transsexual potential of a Bidder's organ represents a fallback position for the toad. If he can't be a male, he re-creates himself as a female to continue a productive life. It's testimony of a slightly different sort from that of the sex-change fish, or of the jack-in-the-pulpit and sea turtle.

Should we assume, therefore, that femaleness stands for maturity in the history of an individual; or perhaps a life of particular warmth and vigor—or a kind of magic fallback permanence that may perpetuate a species? On the other hand, one might argue from these examples that males face more hardship.

205

Luckily, people's psyches seem to include a "Bidder's organ" for both sexes that adds complexity and flexibility and fallback possibilities for human beings.

BANKING
FOR
WINTER

APPLEMEN PRUNE THEIR TREES "so that a crow can fly between any two branches," as the adage goes. And now is the time when they want some apples of the winter varieties, "keepers" for the storage bin. Brussels sprouts, beets, and carrots can still be got from the garden and stored down in the cellar too.

But before there were beets and apples there were beavers—and trappers before farmers. A good trapper hardly needed a rifle to feed himself. His wolf traps would as conveniently catch a deer; his bear traps were just right for moose or buffalo. Mainly, he lived on beavers, and mostly on the tails of the beavers, which were a frontier luxury on a par with buffalo tongues and moose noses.

Beavers rudder or scull themselves, as they swim, with their foot-long, tongue-shaped, broad, scaly tails. They also use the tail to brace themselves as they stand up to gnaw a tree, and as an extra leg for balancing as they clasp mud in their arms and walk upright when dam-building. Warning each other of danger, they whack their tails on the water. The tail provides a means of regulating body temperature in the summer and a place to store fat for the winter.

It was this combination of fat and muscle that made for delicious eating. And now is the time when beavers are stacking poplar branches underwater for winter feeding—ramming them into the mud or piling stones on them to keep them from floating up and freezing in the ice that forms.

For the trapper, all this busy preparation before the ponds closed over added to his own larder as well. The more poplar and birch he saw them haul into the water for winter meals of bark, the fatter he knew their tails were going to grow, to sizzle in his campfire, and the more money John Jacob Astor would pay him for his catch of furs, when he came out of the woods next April.

DECEMBER

DECEMBER SONG

AS AN EXAMPLE OF OUR DIVORCE from nature, the word "creepy" has come to mean behavior most unnatural. Yet if house cats walked as upright as we do—if they didn't creep so magnificently that they remind us of almost the entire world of nature by themselves—we wouldn't have them living with us in every city apartment building. People who do not like cats or dogs keep bowls of Celebes rainbow fish, red snakeskin guppies, calico angelfish, upside down catfish, and Yucatan mollies. And animals in cages would be astounded if one could ever possibly explain to them that the reason they are being held captive is only so that we can *watch* them. (How creepy it would seem!) Though parrots don't talk nearly as sensibly as many of the feeble-minded human beings we choose to institutionalize, other people are willing to pay as much as two or three thousand dollars for the pleasure of a parrot's company. Some marvelous indefinable Amazonian wildness enhances its camaraderie, to the point that many species have been endangered by the pet trade.

Particularly as the winter gathers, we hang Malaysian tree ferns in the window, above a tableful of Sonoran cactus, potted spider grass, and zebra and impatiens plants—impatient ourselves to crowd the narrowest dwelling with green life. Some people buy cut flowers, wreaths, and terrariums in an expansive mood; others fill the house with plants in a bit of panic, as if in December they already feel the walls close in. With houseplants, we reassure ourselves that we, too, will stay green all winter, as in many other ways we are gearing up for the months to come.

December in the woods is an undistinguished time, however. The weather hasn't yet turned bitter or hungry. The deer are through their rutting season, but are still fat from eating apples and beechnuts. Bears and weasels bred early last summer in order to give birth next February and April. Coyotes, coons, and foxes won't mate until about February to meet the same April schedule as the weasels.

Only for the humble porcupine is December a festive month. Porcupines have left the summer greenery of the fields for a winter woodland diet of bark, sheltering under rocks and evergreens. But squalling to each other across the snow, the males and females home in. The male eventually enacts a three-legged nuptial dance before the female while gripping his testicles with one forepaw. For both of them, winter begins on a note of celebration.

ABOUT THE AUTHOR

EDWARD HOAGLAND was born in 1932 and educated at Harvard. He has produced three novels, two travel books and three previous collections of essays: *The Courage of Turtles*, *Walking the Dead Diamond River* and *Red Wolves and Black Bears*. In 1979 a selection of these essays was reissued in *The Edward Hoagland Reader* simultaneously with the publication of his most recent book, *African Calliope: A Journey to the Sudan*, which was nominated for a National Book Critics Circle Award.

Mr. Hoagland divides his time between fiction and essays, and his life between an apartment on the New York waterfront and a house in northern Vermont, where, among other things, he writes nature editorials for the *New York Times*.